The Cowtown Circle

The Cowtown Circle

Poems

Dave Oliphant

ALAMO BAY PRESS
SEADRIFT•AUSTIN

Copyright © 2014, 2016 by Dave Oliphant

All rights reserved. No part of this book may be reproduced in any form without permission in writing from the publisher, except by a reviewer who may quote brief passages in a review.

Cover illustration: *Europa and the Bull* (1943), by Cynthia Brants, a member of the Fort Worth Circle. Permission to reproduce the engraving image granted by the Cynthia Brants Trust, Ron Wenner, T.T.E.E. Special thanks to Cynthia Bell, the Cynthia Brants Gallery and Collections Manager, Granbury, Texas.
Book Design: ABP

For orders and information:
Alamo Bay Press
Pamela Booton, Director
825 W 11th Ste 114
Austin, Texas 78701
pam@alamobaypress.com
www.alamobaypress.com
www.alamobaywritersworkshop.com

Library of Congress Control Number: 2014955241
ISBN: 978-0-9908632-1-2

in memory of
Joseph Evans Slate
(1927-2014)
professor scholar friend

Contents

Lone Star Stalag
- 1   Cedar vs. Live Oak
- 2   Bees & Blue Salvia
- 3   Playing One's Part
- 4   Bunt or Fly Ball
- 5   Austin Autumn
- 7   Running Water
- 10   At the Farmer's Market
- 13   March of the Penguins
- 15   Silverfish
- 16   Of Burgers & Serpents
- 17   After a Brief Illness
- 18   Ode to a '68 VW Bus
- 21   Homeless
- 23   Feelings Near & Far
- 24   Saharan Serendipity
- 25   DeKalb: February 14th 2008
- 27   Bad Day at Black Rock
- 29   Driving Across the Llano Estacado
- 31   Lone Star Stalag

María's Poems
- 37   María's Antiques
- 40   María's Butterflies
- 42   María's Complaint
- 43   María's Crackers
- 45   María's Cross

48 María's Diet
50 María's Ears
52 María's Goodwill
54 María's Heart
56 María's Hem
57 María's Larkspur
60 María's Mask
65 María's Memory
64 María's Movies
69 María's New Mexico
73 María's Paint
75 María's Readings
77 María's Reality
78 María's Redecoration
81 María's Saint
83 María's Smile
86 María's Squirrels
88 María's Treatments
90 María's Wool

On Visiting NYC

95 Donasio Checks the Mail
97 Amaya's "Dixie"
98 Annabella's Art
100 Out on a Limb
102 Girl Gymnasts
103 Udder Delight
104 Oliphant Figurines
107 The Fastest Barber in the West
108 A Grackle's-Eye View of Lakeline Mall
109 After Álvaro Oyarzún's *El autodidacta*
110 On Visiting NYC

Rondo for Mahler
117 Musical & Literary Mementos
119 Boat House Grill
123 Community Music Fest
129 Jazz by the Boulevard
131 Rondo for Mahler

Presidential Doggerel
145 Presidential Doggerel

The Cowtown Circle
163 The Cowtown Circle

Baird
181 The Book's East-Texas Tour
186 Serenading the Neighbors
187 Granny's Dragonflies
189 María's Alstroemeria
191 María's Ideas
193 Baird

219 Acknowledgments
221 About Dave Oliphant

Lone Star Stalag

Cedar vs. Live Oak

neither a law case
nor an athletic game
just a tall straight
trunk against a limb

which came first unclear
whether crooked horizontal oak
preceded furry upright cedar
or conversely neither chokes

the other out one
grows erect to reach
miraculous rays of sun
on other's differing leaves

both green year long
one flat broad ovate
the other a prong
thin pungent pliable pinnate

each unalike in seeds
acorn counters pollen spore
makes the feverish sneeze
its adversary squirrels adore

though not really enemies
just competitors for photosynthesis
on the Hill Country's
hot dry limestone cliffs

preferring either opposes sense
summers need whatever shades
garden or flower-bed fence
requires sturdy enduring stakes

Bees & Blue Salvia

o each day to
be called to one's
honeyed task by clarions
of color & on

sticking tongue in tiny
bell-shaped blooms to hum
the nectar tune buzz
to others & in

flying brush stems will
send to pollinating wings
a rush of fragrance
perfumes air refreshes labor

Playing One's Part

the masked raccoon
hit by a
passing car now

lies beneath this
live-oak tree as
if asleep &

yet it won't
be waking when
on circling down

the buzzard comes
to help keep
up this neighborhood

by performing in
a mournful style
its sanitary blues

Bunt or Fly Ball

    if the one's laid
    down & dribbles out
    of reach of catcher
    pitcher or baseman charging
    in from third even
    if one of those
    throws to first in
    time all the runners
    will've gone by then
    from one diamond facet
    to next equidistant pad
    or at home plate
    have dived or slid
    & if the other
    batted high & far
    enough to right left
    or center so the
    fielder has to wait
    & even if it's
    caught with runners having
    all tagged up &
    taken off the long
    throw or relay may
    arrive too late for
    when a sacrifice works
    another may safely score

Austin Autumn

football weather we call it here
but equally it's welcome relief
from summer's hundred degrees

when at last leaves on crepe myrtles
sumac & Chinese tallow change their colors
from red to yellow pecans falling to squirrels

store them away near a rusting cypress
while sycamore palmates brown & stiffen
flying free till caught in a chain-link fence

& live oak & mountain laurel
green even as the thermometer dips
& the Hill Country begins to freeze

though on campus
coeds still appear
in sandals & sleeveless tops

feet arms shoulders & cleavage
bared to November's bright blue skies
with white wispy clouds or

that gray & overcast tease
brings but a threat of damaging winds
with rain so badly needed

noses itching running &
sneezing from ragweed & later
cedar's exploding seed

if never so glorious as
those maples in Maine
our team's burnt-orange shade

on trees in this season of
wins & losses still a feast
for eyes of every Texas fan

Running Water

with Stage 3 Restrictions in place
from lake levels at historic lows
the chance for rain little or none

feel guilty watering beds & lawn
even with a hand-held hose
yet guilt assuaged somewhat

by the thought in this August heat
of salvia & duranta flowers will feed
bees butterflies & hummingbirds

as the memories now flood back
to the outhouse on that Okie farm
whose family befriended dad

sold them insurance on his
Great American plan an elderly
couple whose tall teenage son

showed me where it was
had never known a home before
without a commode indoors

no toilet paper just Sears
& Roebuck catalogues corn
cobs lying around its hole

cut in rough dry boards
the stink & splashes
risen from far below

then followed him into the barn
told to hold his flashlight
to shine it into the wooden bins

as he aimed & shot his .22
at rats caught within its beam
eating their animals' grain

& later on a daytime visit
shown the tank where
their cows & horses drank

where he & his father fished
for perch mudcat crappie & bass
wondering then

how members of
the "finny tribe"
without a stream

to pour them there
could end up in
their landlocked pond

only push a handle to flush
turn or lift the magic tap
to wash up or take a shower

to rinse the pots & plates
soak roots so plants survive
to nourish creatures fly & suck

at colors soothe the eyes
to insure life on this planet
far more than any policy

Fraternal or Old-Line
Legal Reserve & worth
the fine for letting it flow

more than the permitted
once-a-week though such a

trade-off only differs in kind

from arctic oil
brings plumbing in
with its easy convenient drink

in place of Eskimos hunting
for their communal
subsistence whale

At the Farmers' Market

Saturday mornings by ten
someone rings the bell
for shopping to begin
when local farmers sell

produce out of pickups
spread tomatoes & elephant
garlics on table tops
offer native garden plants

the man from Moody
takes a customer's hand
& rubs it softly
with his special brand

of emu oil guarantees
it'll cure cracked skin
other stands feature cheese
soy flan & German

beef but for kids
the big attraction is
the animals' circus tricks
begin in fifteen minutes

as singing unicyclist balances
& plays his accordion
to announce the performances
including one by Lauren

Bacall the parti-colored parrot
perches upon his shoulder
till every insistent tot
tugs at mother's finger

& pulls her towards
the ringmaster's makeshift tent
with its mongrel barks
of the amazing Chicken

Dog & Jumping Jack
will roll over dance
scratch imaginary fleas act
out parts Darren commands

who feeds them treats
after roles as pirate
or picnicker their feats
most pets can't imitate

but these distracted now
by a purebred passes
near when their trainer-clown
calls "time out" chases

them into his van
switching to a serious
illustration of the lesson
learned in a pre-calculus

class as he lifts
from the plastic bucket's
see-through blue-pink detergent-water mix
strings looped with suds

a breeze slowly inflates
as spheres seek mysterious
equation of greatest space
allowed volume to radius

next his yo-yo exhibition
lets the audience see
how an out-of-work mathematician

The Cowtown Circle

with a bachelor's degree

can walk the dog
& recreate the Eiffel
Tower leaves all agog
then rocks the cradle

joking his mother overdid
it & that's why
he's in this business
earns so little pay

yet clearly it entertains
even the adult crowd
approves skills patience attains
proven by their loud

applause as he juggles
bowling pins & warns
pedestrians while he pedals
& beeps like horns

from honking backing trucks
& at last brings
Lauren on whose trick's
counting by flapping wings

all love her stuff
until a second bite
has him scold "enough's
enough bow good night"

& so in ending
gives his thank-you speech
& to kids bubble-blowing
kits one for each

March of the Penguins

a French film as objective
as the force of life itself
with its sad & splendid

as when at each year's end
emperors in separate gender
lines approach from opposite

compass points on returning
single file to mate again
at the exact same polar basin

as members of monogamous
pairs they recognize one another
from each's remembered call

leaning their affectionate necks
& long beaks pointed upward
as they rub in graceful ballet

later comes the treacherous
transfer of mother's egg
to father's prehistoric feet

before it crack & freeze
while beneath the ice
seals ever swim in wait

for the famished female
will walk for seventy miles
in her short as if skirt-

hindered steps back to
the bountiful deadly sea
to replenish her gullet with

fish will feed their chick
if it hatch beneath the male's
protective feather pouch

as he stands a convict
shackled by the delicate shell
he lifts on his cold-resistant

claw-like nails for over
a hundred days with
no sustenance no relief

shuffling to seek at forty
below the sixty degrees above
found in huddling among

his patient kind
as they gather against
the pitiless Antarctic wind

to preserve the species
in another of this earth's
disturbing amazing displays

Silverfish

    like Melville's whale
    its mermaid tail
    lies flat to

    its finless trunk
    swims in drips
    of faucet-stained sinks

    nibbling spinal sizing
    dust jacket &
    edge of page

    wriggling in the
    gutter's dry sea-roving
    text to catch

    not at meaning
    but glutinous glue
    flour pores printed

    with a poet's
    prose & yet
    may be the

    best-read insect of
    all & perhaps
    of any creature

    as it penetrates
    to the heart
    of Herman's words

Of Burgers & Serpents

how ever have another Big Mac
with double patties & piggy fries
not because her doctor decided
to place his patient on a strict
low-fat low-cholesterol diet
but because her dear child died
from innocent rattlesnake bites

always on passing Golden Arches
or the registered Burger King sign
I think of that San Antonio mother
whose daughter played outside
on the plastic recreational slides
while her mother waited inside
for their fast food soon to arrive

& just before it was ready
she was there beside her mom
sobbing & saying my leg it hurt
where she asked then saw forever
purple bruises the mosquitoes made
believing so when the order came
till her darling girl lay quietly down

on going to inspect the play-set
the manager discovered their nest
disturbed by her sweet little thing
how after that could she ever get on
with the rest of her envenomed life
how ever go on eating or breathing
with those fang marks day & night

After a Brief Illness

Susan Bright is gone
yet still swims on
against the current Development
would pollute & darken
Austin's Barton Springs' pellucid
limestone pool in Plain
View of sacred pecan
& live-oak trees her
poetry written to save

Ode to a '68 VW Bus

for Roger & Tom Funnell

high schoolers pedaling their bikes
& college students in their own or
their daddies' sporty late-model cars

give it in passing the V-fingered sign
as now symbolic it putt-putts along
through shaded neighborhood streets

have even seen a camper-style pictured
in Chile's capital city touring with a living tree
growing right up through its cut-out roof

at the post office one man asked its year
wanted to know how much would sell it for
said his daughter's MS had gotten worse

& to transport her in her powered wheelchair
he'd soon be needing a sliding door
like the dented one on this passenger side

would add a ramp he said but turned him down
how ever put a price on or tell its worth
having shifted it since bicentennial '76

steering it up & around the mountain curves
down through the Mexican tropics
valleys deluged by August monsoons

through humid heat of vast Texas stretches
with their rolling or flat & monotonous plains
their thick pine forests & coastal beaches

had bought it used from an Arlington man

through his ad in the *Fort Worth Star-Telegram*
paid him just seven-fifty & have spent at least

six times as much on upkeep & for overhauling
its four-cylinder air-cooled engine
developed by Adolf's holocaust Nazi regime

though for those remember Woodstock Nixon
& Vietnam it mostly means the hippie movement
with its peace pot-smoking free-love communes

yet to our kids in the '80s just an embarrassment
shamed them so when its unpainted pink-patched
undercoat would appear outside their junior high

carried them & friends to rehearsal or concert
one played bass fiddle another the cello
those the parents couldn't fit into fancy sedans

& when it came time for landscaping the yard
removed its middle seat for flowers & shrubs
shoveled in loam & loaded up garden stones

till its hubcaps nearly touched the pavement
& how forget its serving as storage space
with no more room in the house for tons of books

while the installment-plan-still-unpaid-for-lemon
would fail to run
depended again on this poor old thing

so maligned by the son & daughter
who now fight over who will inherit
its rusted floor-board & unlocking doors

its banged-up bumpers & flaking roof
its driver's side a passing prankster
stained on throwing rotten eggs

but thanks to the mechanics
at Motormania
it still goes rolling right along

Homeless

    array themselves on the steps
    of the Baptist church at Guadalupe
    or seated on the sidewalk

    their backs against a wall
    where Scientology offers
    free Personality Tests

    all dressed in army-surplus camouflage
    as pedestrian eyes try their best
    not to look their way

    at backpacks blankets bare
    feet & mangy dogs but can't
    help wonder how they feed

    their multitude of hungry pets
    all happy as larks even being
    restrained by the leash of city law

    while their masters or mistresses
    seem satisfied just to find a butt
    or receive a dime toward a brown-

    paper bag as they repeat politely
    the same discomfiting line
    Pardon me could you

    spare some change
    & always question
    but never out loud

    would it do more harm than
    good would it make them worse
    or better off with always the guilt-

ridden head-shake keeping
deep in virtuous pockets
the folded bill & lukewarm coin

Feelings Near & Far

she struggles to rise
on her spindly legs
to run & leap once
more beneath the live-oak
trees through the Johnson
grass grown tall enough
by this summer heat
to hide her within
its blades already stained
by her vital fluids
the pavement too where
air-conditioned buses enter &
leave with passengers see
& watch her helpless
& all alone abandoned
by the frightened doe
while a world away
in pools of blood
Iraquis & Afghans lie
wounded from suicide bombs
yet hurt on television
easier to take than
face a dying fawn
is there something wrong
or is it right
to be shaken more
by death up close

Saharan Serendipity

in seeking African dinosaur bones
Sereno & his Chicago team
would come upon their biggest find

they were not even looking for
in an unknown land
filled with corn gold & cacao beans

came across it in Gobero's graves
uncovered by the wind
blowing desert sand

but only if the search is on
can discovery prove of more
than the prehistoric overgrown

a girl with around her thin
surviving wrist an artful hippo ring
a mother with two young sons

drowned in green Sahara's lake
gave them life then took it back
buried with their fingers intertwined

the boys' teeth mixed with flowers
left by those who loved & lost all three
eight millennia later their story told

by patient hands brush the grains away
to preserve with care their dry remains
eyes tearing from the feelings found

ages before recorders in
elegiac poems to set
their own & others' down

DeKalb: 14 February 2008

on Valentine's ten months
after tragedy struck at
Virginia Tech mental illness
took its toll again

here in Illinois heartland
where in Geology class
they jotted down lecture
notes on fractured slate

those five like the
ghost of mobster Jimmy
Clark who haunted Al
Capone begged it Don't

come back to leave
him alone in his
hotel room after that
massacre on love's one

calendar day reappearing here
on this coated stock
of NIU's *Northern Now*
its memorial issue with

their faces forever young
ever hopeful ever aglow
in their ambered photos
even after insanity's gun

had brought an end
to dreamed-of college degrees
to lives dedicated to
each one's chosen field

Bible-reading Gayle to cultural
man attractive Catalina &
Sergeant Julianna to elementary
grades athletic Daniel financial

aid Ryanne counselor to
disturbed had taken aim
never again to tune
or play her violin

Bad Day at Black Rock

drove with Wayne to the Gaylynn Theatre
for viewing in Cinemascope that '55 film
with André Previn's sinister score

the Southern Pacific whistling toward
a dusty adobe town where not one train since '41
had stopped to take on or let off a single soul

not till McCready the one-armed vet
played by Spencer Tracy comes to pay his respects
to a Japanese-American whose son had lost his life

in saving his fellow soldier's the role the actor plays
but the father already murdered by Pearl Harbor hatred
that & the water from a deep well Komoko dug

resented by Robert Ryan as Reno Smith
Ernest Borgnine in the part of the bully whipped
by McCready's cool one-handed jujitsu chops

a totally satisfying flick
then headed for the Pig Stand on Calder Street
for a root beer float to celebrate that very first day

out without an adult along
a big shot in the family car
looking for a place to park

unseeing until too late
a guy backing into that '52 Chevy
when the policeman arrived

& conferred with that older man
who declared we had come
hot-rodding around the corner

as if in sitting still
we could have rammed
his bumper with

the left side door he had dented in
the two men yucking it up
thinking this kid's too young to drive

when to their total surprise
pulled out that brand-new license
yet given a ticket all the same

sent to the juvenile court to listen
& be lectured to as a delinquent
suspended from driving for three long months

by a judge whose daughter
we knew to be the high-school punch
sweet on Wayne & his tennis-team friends

no Spencer there to set things straight
to turn that wrong into
a feel-good Hollywood scene

Driving Across the Llano Estacado

& right away the place names tell the tale
from Earth Sudan & Bovina to Levelland
with ever the next-to-last bringing to mind
Stephen Crane's story his "The Blue Hotel"
whose Cowboy's stupefied to the very end
"bovine" the word that writer assigns to him

between Lubbock & Texas-New Mexico line
feedlots fill the air with their unbearable smell
clanging windmills water the herds by turbine
sprinklers on wheels irrigating flattest of fields
black liquid gold brought up by rusting oil-well
pumps do all such systems signify lower yields

when brains unaware of partners cheat at cards
or do they put them in touch with the elemental
animal mineral the seasons hot cold mostly dry
rounds of plowing & planting crops so often fail
just passing through am amazed they'd even try
living off dust-blown pastures with cattle guards

its weather so unreliable the horizon ever receding to a vanishing point a heat-shimmering lake
a mirage reminds once more of how little comes
of it all with the same tasteless look-alike homes
lawns sun-bleached to straw as musicians weep
over women mistreated keep them wide awake

wonder why for this any would leave wherever
though many did & do today who love to wear
blue jeans & boots at offices the same as rodeo
to dance two-steps to fiddles & whining guitars
underneath a sky lit up at night by myriad stars
birthplace of broncobuster another pigskin hero

still can't understand it & stay dumber than hell
cannot conceive of any choosing to turn up here
even as the son of a father born & raised as near
as twenty miles east of Abilene with his kinsmen
spoke with this same accent have known so well
one day like a needed soaking rain it may sink in

Lone Star Stalag

*after the book by
Michael R. Waters &
his students at Texas A & M*

captured in Tunisia in '43
the POWs made art instead of
lighting up the Arabian skies

with anti-aircraft flak & in place of
following Panzer tracks in
desert sand mixed concrete to cast

a fountain shot
water from mouths of frogs
caught in a platter held by hands

of their sculptured kneeling nude
& cascaded into her cobbled
basin though only now in

distant decades do photos reveal
her stunning face & another of
a six-foot unclothed statue

since only rocks & basin remain
& a pedestal on which she stood
nothing of the braid she pulled

above her breast with head tilted
slightly down in a meditative
pose as she contemplates

what we will never know
although it's clear through her
how her makers thought

of those so faraway
longed for their land recalled
by constructing miniature castles

complete with turrets & moats
with one flew a swastika flag
since some not all believed in the end

Hitler was bound to win
one remembered his journey here
& engraved in his aluminum

his standard-issue canteen
the scene of a veiled Muslim
with a water jug upon her head

followed by a turbaned man
both beneath a palm a gate-
way arch with a mosque nearby

& into the metal's oval edge
scratched the cities he'd passed en route
Palermo Tunis Casablanca

Pittsburgh New York
Philly & St. Louie
then etched on the other side

the guard tower overlooking
barracks & barbed-wire fence
& below them in printed letters

HEARNE TEXAS
U.S.A.
PRISONER OF WAR

while another drew himself
behind the twisted strands

with his number underneath

his eyes a dark resistant stare
one painted seascapes
another sculpted from mortar

ships & a cross-legged man
wearing a cowboy hat
a hole in his hand for holding

a rod & reel
others erected a music shell
for performances by their captive band

musicians once under
Wilhelm Furtwängler
had played Beethoven & Wagner

here led by Willi Mets
conductor in years before
of the Leipzig philharmonic

a few staged operettas
sewed their own costumes
designed the sets themselves

delivering lines had learned
in remembered civilian days
while a few could not forget

their loyalty to the Führer
their duty to the Fatherland
& so with nails in sticks

battered to death
one among their own
they knew was not a Nazi

while three escaped to discover
the vastness of this State
its Brazos River too low to float

their raincoat-fashioned kayak
the trio welcomed at Christmas time
by a farm family invited them in

for dinner with all the trimmings
till caught by the sheriff's men
what moral to draw if any

for in every time & place
war & art have ever been
& though some men destroy

others in whatever form
seek wherever they are
creative joy

María's Poems

María's Antiques

would need no dealer
to judge their worth
no auctioneer to call

for an opening bid
on her buck bow
saw with its symmetrical

wooden cheeks held in
tension by its rusted
turnbuckle parallel to the

length of its rusty
teeth had given next
to nothing for when

the neighbor held his
moving sale not for
lopping off branch or

limb but to hang
its wide H upon
the kitchen wall to

rest its longer handle
along the frame of
the adjacent bedroom door

for who would make
an offer on her
padlock without a key

purchased in a Chilean
store whose owner listed
on a sign the

amount of time he
would give to customers
& compadres none to

those with "bright ideas"
two hours to those
invited to lunch more

to those had come
to buy or pay
her latest from two

doors down at an
estate sale run by
the elderly lady's surviving

son carried the lawn
mower here with its
wheels no longer roll

its push handle now
leans against the backyard
fence no grass to

cut just her shrubs
& flowers in beds
& red clay pots

her collectibles rated at
less than she paid
but more to her

for materials & shapes
the lives they touched
& were needed by

for their stainless blades
or their protective steel

kept their treasures safe

valued most for just
themselves not so much
for any use they

had or yet may
serve but rather their
meaning mainly lies in

taking her back in
time to golden moments
they still can lend

to her her family
& friends while best
of all her relics

keyed unlocked & lubricated
these lines for appraising
her heart & mind

María's Butterflies

because they are only
passing through they won't
be staying long doesn't
know their Latin names

just recognized by their
pattern & size the
smallest of all a
pale-yellow had spotted before

swarming here from Mexico
smeared on windshields &
grills by speeding cars
unfluttering on asphalt lanes

nor can she tell
the type of bush
surely a sage with
woody stems & serrated

leaves attracts their weightless
wings more than any
brighter colors any stronger
or subtler scent though

this one's flowers bluer
than the one out
back with its blooms
of a lighter shade

unlike them she herself
has stayed on through
every season of unbearable
heat cedar fever &

even my exaggerated fits
when afterwards like the
orange-&-black had lit on
her I'm drawn to

settle down on finding
she offers as ever
fragrant delectable nectar as
freely as blossoms give

María's Complaint

is not the
one 19th-century medical
men came up

with on diagnosing
women as hysterical
& weak such

physicians prescribed for
them no exercise
just rest isolation

& opium since
hers rather concerns
my being in

her clever conceit
an ivory-billed woodpecker
some contend does

not exist this
one upstairs in
his ivory tower

tapping away at
his keyboard while
downstairs she's watching

television & for
the sightings few
& far between

María's Crackers

is a title only
happens to play upon
the fact she's crazy

about this orange tabby
named by the neighbor's
late New Jersey mother-in-law

whom the daughter-in-law it
seems disliked as she
did him whom I

have called a Georgia
crack-cocaine from the addiction
he has caused &

the cost after Blackie
had bitten his left
front leg abscessed until

he couldn't walk so
had to carry him
to Dr. Kim the

female vet who beneath
his coat found a
chip in his skin

identified his owner as
that awful woman who—
for having rejected her

adopted ring-tailed darling pet
wakes us up in
the middle of the

night jumping onto the
bed (not to mention
the bill for surgery

antibiotics & a rabies
shot) & for not
having offered to pay

—will one day she
tells her bratty cat
surely burn in hell

María's Cross

besides at times the
one I've been for
her to bear another

is made of pine
lacquered black with on
its horizontal & vertical

beams straw cut in
minute diamond shapes &
appliquéd in patterns of

eight-point star-like flowers with
a single petal in
between & each pattern

a quadrilateral arranged in
fours or sixes &
balanced down or across

eight-point star-like flowers with
a single petal in
between & each a

quadrilateral arranged in either
fours or sixes &
balanced down or across

the humble cruciform with
its elaborate & delicate
floral design centered upon

its pair of timbers
all this the patient
work of Diana Lujan

purchased in Corrales at
the folk-art market of
Old San Ysidro Church

dates from 1868 its
cracked adobe walls shining
with yellow flecks of

summer & winter hay
harvested from simple grasses
oat barley timothy &

the wheat of gold
split sliced & glued
in a traditional Spanish

way brought back by
Eliseo Rodríguez during WPA
he a "New Mexican

Treasure" she had to
visit to see his
roods so exquisite in

rooms he built himself
already she had viewed
in Santa Fe his

life-sized tableau & too
his wife Paula's beauteous
santos but she ill

in bed while he
at 92 still happy
to show & tell

as his fan snapped

pictures & asked him
how he'd recovered this

lost religious art &
later photographed on the
plaza walk a bronze

plaque celebrates the man
whose crucifix she all
but worships with its

stations each of straw

María's Diet

no physician she had seen
here in the capital city
of this Lone Star State

could find any reason for
the aches & pains in
her every joint arms legs

back & neck or why
when she walked her feet
went snap crackle & pop

ran every kind of test
sent her to a physical
therapist declared her muscles limp

tried to "pump them up"
but neither exercises nor lifting
weights nothing would bring relief

not until she traveled to
her native land & saw
Dr. Silva a Chilean who

by peering into her iris
& glimpsing signs no x-rays
ever reveal diagnosed her fibromyalgia

his practice not limited to
traditional cures but including hot
wet towels cold mud packs

herbal teas but most of
all her vegan meals no
meat fish eggs or cheese

her friends asking her how
can anyone live like that
on salad fruit & veggies

in reply would tell them
long ago Thoreau her hero
wrote cows survive on grass

but if she herself cannot
neither can she taste again
eggplant baked with olive oil

or Irish potato wrapped in
foil since the two contain
solanine can cause arthritic pain

debilitates by poisoning connective tissue
yet now she's doing fine
thanks to food she never

consumes & to her countryman
spied & identified symptomatic motes
with his beamless medical eye

María's Ears

are a little
larger than some
& will if

they care to
listen better than
most & through

them can whistle
any pop-song tune
or movie theme

even whole sections
of symphonies they
once have heard

at night removes
her earrings from
lobes pierced at

birth & propped
up by her
pillows begins to

read when then
I hum &
um-yum-yum on nibbling

upon soft &
delicious tips the
only bedtime sounds

am permitted to
make since these
cannot compete with

her concentrating on
another writer's words
whisk her away

to where to
such caresses they're
both stone deaf

María's Goodwill

used donations prices lower
policy of hiring handicapped
these brought her here
for plates to catch

water from potted indoor
plants as I listen
in this sun-warmed car
to the classical station

its early music ballad
after a Decameron tale
of Abbess who had
gotten caught the wimple

not hers as knock
at door would discover
her dishabille her shock
at underwear of lover

then noticing the store
name across its sign
repeated over & over
in one continuous line

I shuffle the letters
of the words combined
& find thirty others
form questions & rhymes:

will good do ill
low gold glow idol
old wid woo lil
wool wig gill doll

dill log lid wold
wood oil gild goo
owl god go wild
loo dog dig igloo

if Boccaccio in translation
has word order changed
is the language newfangled
or still but secondhand

such concerns of course
were none of hers
who had in mind
flowers watered in wintertime

yet whatever she's needed
has nourished poetry's leaves
fed roots & seeded
singing's parts of speech

María's Heart

    (or whichever organ it is
    hurts from what we miss)
    bears the tiniest tear
    in the shape of where
    she was born to be
    in her long thin native Chile
    given up against her will
    once love had made her feel
    through affection's forceful sway
    she must forsake it & come away
    to this foreign place as any African slave
    or more like the poor & oppressed still brave
    immigrant hardship as did the Irish & Russian Jews
    but those of their own volition would choose
    to take the risk & make the voyage
    in a cramped unhealthful steerage
    if surviving to land on Ellis Island
    arriving barely to understand
    the official exam would undergo
    if answered wrong stamped mentally slow
    deported alone separated from parents whose family name
    anglicized by authorities & on Galveston Isle the same
    quarantined & lined up all in the nude
    for delousing by inspectors whose forebears earlier sued
    to enter the Redman's space any indignity ready to endure
    since each & every self so wonderfully sure
    in its innocent soul (or whatever it is
    suffers pain for future bliss)
    it would soon find freedom's hope fulfilled
    but with her longing for home unstilled
    the rip from that rift now throbs again
    its wound yet seeping deep within
    & all because her coming here
    cut her off from a relationship first & forever dear
    her maiden name replaced by mine

a Scottish on paperwork she has had to sign
on her alien card rude agents review with every trip
since she won't surrender her Chilean citizenship
& how does it make me feel
her having come against her will
o torn in two though in the end
know she's stayed & as yet no law has passed to send
her back & so have tried to believe it's right
in the Logic-versus-Emotion title fight
the decision should go to the breakable heart
(if that's the body's loving irrational part)

María's Hem

before my barefoot contessa
will baste by hand & sew
she has me measure all around

from bottom of skirt to table top
where her seductive feet now
slowly turn

to this pinning marks
the proper length
as I kneel before this table

like the pedestal I have ever
placed her on
though to her it's just

pure sacrilege
can hear her say
they're made of clay

& yet love needles
until once more
impiety sings

her inch by
inch another
fitting hymn

María's Larkspur

a variety called
Cloudy Skies who
knows why when

its bloom's no
fluffy cumulus but
a spurred calyx

of pink violet
blue or white
prefers rich well-drained

soil ample water
will not the
catalog ads declare

rain on your
day yet does
dislike to be

transplanted & looks
best in patches
clustered together though

unseen in the
backyard where she
set them out

& yet from
there a gully-washer
would sweep their

seeds away &
ending up in
front between sidewalk

& curb they
rooted in dirt
under pea-sized gravel

her *Delphinium consolida*
a genus complex
as orchids although

absent any genetic
barrier to intercrossing
its hybridizing has

brought such comfort
as when this
month after the

deep winter freeze
had done in
her white dewdrop

duranta whose blossoms
draw butterfly bee
& hummingbird these

lifted their sepals
stamens styles anthers
pedicels & pistils

& for decades
the description says
will yield a

steady petal supply
& not for
her eyes alone

since just last
week two young

girls white &

black knelt on
this asphalt street
the latter snapping

a photograph for
lack perhaps of
beauty at home

carried their picture
to share it
with those may

have needed the
sight even more
if only as

a Kodacolor &
though the real
thing brown &

wither will yet
return with spring
& while too

my flower who
sowed them first
must fade as

any blossom her
stigmas left behind
will on another

day in receiving
pollen germinate her
bright consoling clouds

María's Mask

    each night she slips
    its white elastic band
    over her head &

    behind her now gray
    hair with in its
    blue-green satin finish no

    slits for eyes not
    to masquerade not to
    hide & go unrecognized

    but to keep from
    being awakened through curtain
    or blind by the

    peeping moon streetlight or
    my too-bright Texas sun
    for when she is

    she can't fall back
    asleep & must read
    or arise & begin

    her chores even at
    four a.m. although has
    yet to come to

    earplugs against my snores
    when I roll over
    onto my back or

    turn to her side
    to blow like a
    breaching whale disrupts her

beauty rest her dreams
I'll never sound her
deepest self have never

known can only spy
her lovely lips release
her Chilean tones whistled

Beethoven or Dylan tunes
or early music for
Arabian oud & once

removed the eyes it
reveals ever steal &
harpoon this heart again

María's Memory

    her short-term is not
    what once it was
    though it's long still
    on the distant past

    what happened this morning
    or just last night
    or the day before
    it may not recall

    but from childhood in
    rainy Temuco it retains
    Lautaro the street named
    for Ercilla's Araucanian chief

    on it too Pablo
    Neruda lived & also
    saw *La Bota roja*
    its shoemaker's red-boot sign

    from summer vacations spent
    in La Chimba with her
    Aguirre kin she remembers
    avocado & walnut trees

    & still quotes the
    Jonathan Winters lines of
    wife returning merchandise sold
    to her "milk-toast" mate

    "Hello STORE it's ME!"
    pinning the salesman down
    & forcing him to
    repeat "Customer's always right"

nor forgets politically incorrect
Seinfeld sitcom scenes of
parking in handicapped space
stealing senior's babka cake

always reminded by such
of the dumb things
I've said or done
the letter published led

to a Federal case
unwise decisions acted upon
before had checked with
her but good times

too as when after
25 years vows renewed
to love & cherish
in sickness & health

María's Movies

are none she's made herself
only those she has seen
again & again her all-time

favorite *Captain & Commande*r with
Russell Crowe even though she's
so opposed to violence in

life & film but can
allow it on the screen
if acting writing & cinematography

all come together as when
from his crew's cello-playing naturalist-physician
that Aussie actor learns of

an insect camouflaged as stick
or twig & disguises their
outmanned vessel as a blubber-smoking

whaler takes by complete surprise
the superior Napoleonic warship &
high too on her list

actor-director Warren Beatty as Jack
Reed in *Reds* with Diane
Keaton as Louise Bryant asks

as what would she go
with him to NYC his
wife or concubine his reply

with Thanksgiving near why not
come as a turkey with
Jack Nicholson as cynical playwright

Gene O'Neill & Henry Miller
historical witness to Communist dreams
observing with one eye closed

as much fucking went on
then as now but today
it's perverse while those showed

a bit of heart &
even love & she also
gets a kick out of

John Cusack in *High Fidelity*
with its top-ten pop-song themes
Jack Black as the record-store

clerk dresses a customer down
for his collection doesn't include
Bob Dylan's *Blonde on Blonde*

& of course Marisa Tomei
as an out-of-work hairdresser whose
biological clock's ticking away while

Joe Pesci her lawyer-fiancé knows
no court-room procedure together in
My Cousin Vinny whose witty

script with its details like
mud in tires & cooking
grits seem only meant for

laughs but return as significant
facts & win the case
for two students wrongly accused

yet mostly she prefers to

the Hollywood epic or comic
routine such foreign-made features as

The Syrian Bride who's stopped
at the border crossing &
kept from joining her unknown

groom by the Israelis &
her own Islamic guards &
were she to leave would

not be permitted ever again
to return to her country
& this my Chilean understands

from having given up her
native land for this marriage
could've gone wrong is still

resented by her countrymen for
marrying a gringo & agreeing
to go abroad with him

& suspicious here from never
becoming a citizen but ever
remaining year-after-year a registered alien

& in *The Weeping Camel*
identifies deeply with its ceremony
performed in the Mongolian Gobi

for the mother after her
difficult birth won't feed her
own white colt until with

his two-stringed horse-head fiddle the
musician sings *hoos hoos hoos*
pleading with notes & words

for her to accept her
hungry offspring cries each morning
to suckle her nourishing milk

& adores *The Vertical Ray
of the Sun* with its
three Vietnamese daughters prepare their

parents' memorial banquet while each
in her way unhappy &
yet all beautifully affectively shot

one with a husband with
writer's block another whose spouse
visits his lover in his

other house the unwed youngest
living with her brother &
fantasizing she carries a child

or those like the Israeli
Lemon Tree pictures the injustice
of their Supreme Court ruling

against the Palestinian's grove on
upholding its being bulldozed down
or *Bliss* the gripping Turkish

flick of the innocent girl
secretly raped by the village
leader demands an honor killing

sends his son to pull
the trigger or force her
into a suicide leap but

fallen in love with her
he comes to hide her

till the truth will out

& the lives in *Cave*
of the Yellow Dog &
The Scent of Green Papaya

most of all in *Once*
with its music & love
sung & playacted from life

by Glen Hansard the Irish
singer & Markéta Irglová his
gorgeous Czech immigrant friend these

half-fictions real to her not
TV reality shows but more
like documentaries on rented DVDs

María's New Mexico

ever begins at the end
of the Santa Fe Trail
where trappers settlers & traders

after their thousand-mile overland trek
cheered & tossed their bonnets
beaver caps & broad-brimmed hats

high in the autumn air
on looking down at last
from the Sangre de Cristo's

snow-mantled peaks & glimpsing sight
of cottonwoods & aspens below
with leaves richer than even

Cíbola's gold their yellows Gustave
Baumann later engraved & other
artists minted in modernist oils

the Plaza where native craftsmen
display their rings & necklaces
silver & turquoise with squash-blossom

& bear-claw tabs mosaic inlay
pendants spread out on cloths
along the Governor's Palace walls

across from the sidewalk plaques
honor Georgia O'Keeffe Eliseo Rodríguez
Willa Cather Oliver La Farge

yet unlike the weary &
relieved she stops here only
briefly before she continues north

on the high road to
Chimayó Truchas Trampas & Peñasco
but Taos most of all

by that scenic route with
its poverty & collapsing homes
next to pricey gallery art

or will take the Rio
Grande drive to Embudo &
Velarde by apple orchards at

Dixon past Stanley Crawford's garlic
farm with roadside stands offer
red chile ristras & in

spring rafters running rapids although
she never comes for sports
just heads for Mabel's hom

& Couse's too to walk
again the former's grounds to
observe their surrounding trees &

their dovecote pigeons circle around
on gray-white wings to take
in against the clear blue

sky the sacred mountain Mabel
viewed from her upstairs room
for years has wished to

see inside where Brett &
the prudish Lorenzo painted the
bathroom window or on oppressive

summer days where Mabel drank
her lemonade the cozy winter

fireplace where she awaited return

of her wise & regal
Tony & comes to watch
the acequia ripple beneath a

footbridge near the hand-carved gate
saved from the Ranchos church
after the French archbishop unhinged

& removed its rustic doors
replaced them in the town's
now most illustrious tourist attraction

its sight etched painted &
photographed so many times from
not the front but the

bare backside's curved adobe slope
& must explore every nook
& cranny in the studio

where Couse would work upon
his fireside scenes with his
models either of Pueblo brothers

as if his own his
homage paid to their dignified
race & she's enamored too

of hand-cut beams & of
stone-filtered water she savors still
from Chilean summers recovered here

in this Indian-Hispanic-Anglo state with
its past to which she
feels akin since its Chama

& chamisa return her to
her youthful days in La
Chimba's dry & fruitful land

whose longed-for time & place
she visits again if only
through a museum exhibit case

María's Paint

after a novel by W.D. Howells

its label claims one easy coat's enough
to do the job as deodorant & patriotism
she calls the great American cover-ups
hide sweaty odor & a multitude of sins

but first she insists I'll have to clean
with bleach & remove the grime before
I apply the light & darker green
picked from samples the hardware store

gave her free of charge she like Lapham's
wife determined to have the colors
changed on all the outside walls & trim
tired of seeing on windows & doors

the same ugly grayish brown so common
here in Texas where that protagonist came
then returned to rise & fall in his own
Vermont where Pert whose dearest name

he gave to his line of fancy shades
goaded Silas until he set a date & got
it done while week after week have just delayed
the inevitable by resisting in cold or hot

as the brand she bought or the one
he sold from a rotten-tree mine his father
had lucked upon as I still put off the bother
of masking tape of loading the caulking gun

of climbing a ladder unreaches to gable tops
with enamel dropping in dribs & drips
on bifocals shirt pants sandals & sox

then washing rollers brushes & stirring sticks

even as she assures me once I finish
I'll feel so virtuous & will love the fresher
look & this is true though any real pleasure
will only come from giving her her wish

María's Readings

run circles around my own
everything from *Walden* &
Mayordomo to endless articles
ferreted out on the Internet

before it was novels in French
but not anymore & except for
Little Women her favorite since
her teens it's all non-fiction now

always she reads a bit each night
to help her fall asleep her head
nodding & then jerking back up
as once more she tries to finish

the same sentence then gives
it up after her book drops off
the side of the bed & has lost
her page & the bookmark too

the best part's when she reads to
me a paragraph she always loves
from Mabel Dodge Lujan's *Winter
in Taos* of Tony the Indian who

showed her his enchanted land
where to find an antique trunk
works I would not have thought
to look into like *Turn Left at the

Sleeping Dog* learning through her
how garlic is grown & of the Old
Lyme home of Florence Griswold
rented to American impressionists

with their Connecticut scenes of
painted trees sails on the clouded
sea by Willard Metcalf collector of
bird nests & colored speckled eggs

just such delicate things on earth
the subjects of second-hand books
friends she lives with on intimate
terms caressing not caring if she

bends their backs even wets them
in her bath as juice from orange
apple or pear runs down her chin
the unread poet can't wait to kiss

María's Reality

every day she faces it squarely
not one to seek the easy way out
but lives with mosquitoes & snakes
unknown to her in her native land

when doctors diagnosed the cancer
she reviewed her life without regret
if ending then saw it filled with love
her own for others & theirs for her

though tired of cooking healthy meals
she fixes vegan dishes her diet requires
does without sugar eggs milk cheese &
meat—doesn't miss them just broiled fish

believes the hoped-for we don't receive
proves oftenest to have been for the best
not passive nor complacent nor indecisive
is ready & willing to accept & take the test

thrives & blooms as her pretty plumbago
even in this Texas summer's sweltering heat
although unlike that flower she's never blue
yet does prefer overcast to this blinding light

her dreams never unreal but take the form
of a simple desire to visit Taos in autumn
see her own grown children both succeed
her grandchildren turn out as happy as she

whether it's waking or sleeping or speaking
English or her Chilean Spanish even hearing
her on the phone tell her sister I never listen
to a word she says it's the daily dose I need

María's Redecoration

    comes twice a year
    when with spring &
    fall she changes to

    seasonal shades as do
    skies grass & leaves
    repaints the shelves &

    replaces light-green plates or
    blue-on-white with the yellow
    autumnal set & then

    rearranges furniture in the
    living room & washes
    starches irons & fits

    homemade covers on garage-sale
    finds her sofa couch
    & cheap love seat

    takes down & alternates
    framed prints & exhibit
    posters with mostly Santa

    Fe & Taos themes
    her impressionist Connecticut scenes
    or her favorite Matisse

    of a young woman
    sits with a blank
    book upon her lap

    substitutes a displayed copy
    of Thoreau's *Maine Woods*
    river trips for his

Wild Fruits moves antique
crocks from above the
pantry to cabinet tops

brings back sailboats dry-docked
in closet or garage
to launch them on

the mantel again its
fireplace rarely used in
this Texas weather removed

when her keen nose
detected the reek of
rat droppings in nests

of its pink fluffy
insulation for must have
every six months a

different look to keep
mind & eyesight fresh
while I a creature

of habit complain but
then on giving in
lift cart & resort

to the brutish force
she's ever against although
she will allow it

as a necessary helpful
ill & in the
end I must admit

such exertion does renew
the spirit but mostly

the getting to see

her creative touch with
the old decor is
all it takes to

learn change is better
than same except for
this year-round loving her

María's Saint

is none she
depends upon to
intercede & answer

any fervent prayer
not being one
to pray nor

even to believe
angels ever hitched
San Isidro's oxen

& plowed the
field for him
though what goes

on inside her
pretty little head
as on that

'40s radio show
only the Shadow
knows can just

be certain she
loves his picture
as farmer gardener

& bringer of
rain will end
the drought &

ensure the harvest
his bearded booted
haloed likeness pasted

onto a piece
of tin with
flowers or stars

or decorative patterns
hammered around its
printed paper another

of tin on
the bedroom wall
& he's also

on a postcard
purchased from the
Santa Fe Museum

of Spanish Colonial
Art now rests
upon her bookshelf

all remind what
a saint she's
been to put

up with the
poems she says
have exploited her

María's Smile

has never changed with
age the welcoming curve
of her winsome lips
two front teeth first

glimpsed in Santiago's Institute
at the check-out desk
as she stamped due
dates filled patron requests

happy in her work
searching file & record
always ready to serve
but ID card required

can recognize it anywhere
in profile years before
standing among stone layers
broken in Chile's north

with her left foot
tiptoed & her face
with its ingenuous look
turned from barren space

toward the camera lens
the scarf she wears
knotted beneath her chin
homemade skirt & sweater

captured at sixteen in
copper country by Saul
an admirer from then
grateful to that rival

for his earlier lust
inscribed on this picture
his "She at Dusk"
"*Ella en un Atardecer*"

after our wedding giving
birth & writing kin
desperately missed on living
in places ever alien

on a teacher's pathetic
pay then returned together
to visit Arica's Pacific
coast with behind her

banana leaves & waves
she in yellow sweatshirt
& red corn-kernels necklace
so beautiful it hurt

her hairline straight between
dark strands combed apart
pulled back by ribbon
a rubber band starts

thoughts again of how
her mature dignified style
she insists on now
has replaced that idyll

refuses to play her
younger self to dress
as if a teenager
then gaze at this

of a second grandchild
held in her arms
here too her smile

remaining just as warm

tender open if anything
even sweeter no gray
untinted hair no wrinkling
taking its radiance away

María's Squirrels

    visit the bird feeder
    whenever they feel the
    need & over her
    passionate protests take their

    flying leaps even in
    spite of chicken wire
    nailed to grape-arbor boards
    sticking their perfect landings

    on her red-metal roof
    then clawing out sunflower
    seeds clinging by one
    paw reaching with another

    so infuriating to her
    with their lack of
    any sense of what
    is right & proper

    ugly little rats with
    bushy tails is all
    they mean to her
    who drive away her

    blue jays her brightly-colored
    cardinal males her brown-toned
    females in loving pairs
    even to tell her

    they too must eat
    it makes no difference
    they she only declares
    must learn their place

where that is she
never says but maybe
in pecan trees somewhere
else or digging into

pot plants in another's
yard so long as
they do not bury
their acorns in hers

unlike them am fortunate
to be allowed to
stay the same as
all her pampered birds

even if I have
misbehaved been inconsiderate as
grackles she hates &
those pesky irksome rodents

María's Treatments

pain in her neck & all her joints
led her to the ancient Chinese art
of needles in ears & at vital points

& to try chiropractic for nerves
pinched by disks deteriorated in
her backbone's scoliotic curves

warped vertebras one leg slightly
shorter though such conditions
remain unseen with her beauty

ever unchanged ever her same
delicious self but then from
so many tender spots became

an untouchable from her fear
my caresses could harm & I an outcast
was not permitted to come too near

or to stroke or pet for only
her doctor allowed to massage
stretch bend & gently

twist her precious limbs
the acupuncturist to tune
& soothe her tendons

for if soaking her aching
connective tissue with
Epsom salt could bring

a bit of relief professional men
did more with fingers trained
to feel her bones & velvet skin

to rub or press as I'd sit outside
in their antiseptic waiting rooms
she on their office beds inside

pinned or manipulated to realign
so chi energy might flow again
up & down the beloved spine

María's Wool

never has she pulled any
over my eyes nor ever
indulged in idle dreams just

gathers skeins tinted apple green
from natre (an Araucana's voice)
fern   winter bark   shawl of

Eve & palqui leaves whose
odor isn't nice & yet
from them an ointment salves

insect bites & their color
lends a subtle shade to
yarn from Lipimávida two words

in the Mapudungun tongue *lipi*
feather & *mávida* mount name
that town whose Pacific waves

roll endlessly in on beaches
where after earthquake in 2010
tsunami wrecked their summer resorts

but to her the place
mostly means a home with
dogs ducklings & children at

play of the man dyed
the fiber & sold it
to her no tall tale

of rocky ledge's magic wings
take flight & carry youth
& maiden to safe escape

from those oppose their love
but soft warm balls have
granted to this distant room

a touch of her longed-for
aromatic land unlike that Mapuche
legend with its trickster lore

since never has she once
deceived yet she beguiled by
me begged until she'd leave

forsake her towering eucalyptus trees
her Andean snow & come
with me to this flat

all-but scrubby State not knowing
here she would live without
those sights & aromas still

so dear yet given up
for me & now each
day each year she's stayed

has knitted her pungent native
plants with this regret &
gladness this remorse & gratitude

On Visiting NYC

Donasio Checks the Mail

at not quite two
he's in no hurry
to fetch the cards
letters or brochures from

companies or persons mean
nothing to him names
he may have heard
but seen he cannot

read mostly goes for
stops along the way
to pick up leaves
oak elm sycamore in

distinctive shapes & shades
to him no news
compares with birds he
spots in neighbors' bare-limbed

trees thrilled more by
dog cat or bushy-tailed
squirrel than any dull
gas or electric bill

or catalogs offer super
sales on gadgets as
yet he cannot work
or the latest fashions

with none in his
own size but happy
to carry pizza ads
to mom & dad

always eager to hold
to granddad's hand when
his sister turning four
prefers to stay at

home & play with
dolls or view her
videos & won't be
long till he too

finds it all a
bore bearing with a
slow old man has
nothing better to do

than hope for other
than another notice of
payment due instead of
rejection an acceptance slip

yet just to see
him relish the walk
brings tidings more timely
than stamped canceled envelopes

Amaya's "Dixie"

she works each day to
have it come out right
going over it once again
on this converted player piano
not knowing its history from

blackface minstrel to Civil War
just the tune & when
her fingers fail to hit
the proper keys & swing
the rhythm even Lincoln loved

its lyrics she perhaps has
heard & even if not
forgotten the land of picked
back-breaking cotton can hardly mean
a thing to her who's

never seen a boll nor
heard a person pine to
return to where he or
she was born to endure
indignity morning noon & night

she's only concerned to read
& make the notes printed
on paper sheets sound happy
& free from every mistake
will gain her teacher's praise

Annabella's Art

after she's babied her doll
as if it were real
& changed its diapers

like those her mommy
changed for her
she draws with chalk

on driveway & walk
such images as
sunflower cat & fish

the last complete with
seaweed & then on a bio-
degradable tablet sheet

creates with crayons
creatures in colors have
not been seen & even

with just her finger
traces head tail
paws & whiskers in

the upstairs carpet newly
installed from her
need to know or to

make them all come true
on pavement paper or
synthetic nap

through a natural craft
will last even after
she's back at home

with her mom & dad
or at least until we run
the vacuum cleaner

or rainstorms wash her
sketches away though a
few have safely framed

Out on a Limb

though short at four-years-old
it is easy enough
on this park playground
for Annabella to climb

a live oak with
its low crotch formed
of a double trunk
grown half perpendicular half

into a horizontal limb
she stretches out upon
turning about as fingers
grip the bark &

with feet & bottom
caterpillars backwards above the
imaginary sea as Isabella
yells "Don't fall Sharks

will eat you alive"
when Anna holds to
a vertical branch &
pulls herself up as

Issa directs her to
jump down onto grass
not the shaded earth
changed for the game

to water's dangerous depth
& so she does
then awaits her turn
to climb again after

Issa takes her own
when Anna ventures out
farther than before &
her weight lowers the

limb though not in
reach of snapping teeth
but of two swash-buckling
brats who hack the

tree till one sword
nicks her bare little
leg & makes her
cry yet is saved

by Issa who in
helping her down keeps
her head from threatening
waves & all the

while tells them off
"You mean & awful
boys You hurt my
sister Go away" shouts

"You do not even
know how to play"
may they live to
regret they bullied her

dream forever of being
knighted on bended knees
by this queen of
all their lonely nights

Girl Gymnasts

before these pre-teens can cartwheel
& bend on the rail-like balance beam
do handstands & scissor their lifted legs

do a split & after a double or triple flip
stick a landing on steady heels & toes
must first raise their arms & fingers

& ready themselves for tucking heads
on leaping diving & curving torsos
with only their feet to touch the floor

& those precisely on this carpet tape
the same width as that narrow beam
preparation for artful athletic routines

but higher acts with distance between
them & the surface of Wininger's gym
as now they practice on its wider space

bumping again their young little buns
in putting into action a phrase written
out on the entryway's dry-erase board

"Triumph is just 'umph' added to 'try'!"
aspiring not so much to ribbon or trophy
as to overcome what keeps them from

daring to defeat with the mind & body
a fear of falling or of failing to execute
each exercise with ease & natural grace

Udder Delight

taste buds
still recall
from that
onetime ice-cream
shop those
heaped servings
of fruit
& natural
flavors while
brain retains
& savors
its witty
dairy name

Oliphant Figurines

line the bookcase single file
in front of volumes cloth
& paper with one includes
cummings' "earth's most terrific quadruped"
& another Marianne Moore's "both

jewel and jeweler in the
hairs that he wears" although
the Viking *Reader* excludes her
best-known poem with its allusion
to the creature's inexplicable "pushing"

brings back that boyhood circus
where within its sawdust ring
real ones paraded trunk-to-tail as
trainers pulled on metal hooks
caught in their enormous ears

evolved for cooling down their
massive frames yet these are
miniatures except for the biggest
a gift the Baynhams bought
at a 10,000 Villages shop

none in this room ignored
not one an unwanted white
the soldered tin with India-styled
ringleted feet returns Fats Waller's
song of her "colossal pedal

extremities . . . gunboats!" a sound like
"baby elephant patter" as if
from the smallest of all
a lavender-pink plastic the rest
varied in size shape &

substance from tufted to pale-green
origami a pair of tannish
milky onyx teeny & taller
the latter's ivory-colored tusks inserted
or glued not thankfully poached

seven were carved from wood
three of darker browns with
on their backs carpets painted
in decorative gold one with
trunk curled under & up

at the zoo recall their
skin's soft touch snuffing from
outstretched palm those popcorn puffs
nothings compared to 300 daily
pounds of their staple bamboo

shoots of which grow from
water in Lorenzo's bowl around
whose edge three pachyderm heads
seem with each one's glazed
proboscis to suck their fill

even though there's hardly enough
to supply the proverbial drop
in their 25-gallon-per-day drinking bucket
not counting waterholes dug to
wallow in & spray bathe

the reason for this herd
of mammals it's said will
never forget but ever grieves
for memorial bones of their
kind though not even kin

their memories stored in huge
hearts & brains is just

because friends & relations gave
each replica piece to honor
from them my Old-French name

carries a symbolism of chastity
& reincarnation & while reportedly
they're afraid of mice Lion
Kings only attack their calves
hyena & hippo steering clear

eastern religions proclaim their year
politicians too though the Grand
Old Party aside from Abe
& Teddy has rarely followed
their empathic example poets extol

The Fastest Barber in the West

is Sophia who bills herself as such
with her mirror's lipstick-written sign
whose cheap price can't be beat

just six ninety-nine for a buzz
with electric clippers & a snipping
around the ears or a lowering them

as they used to say all so quick
there's hardly time for taking in
the soap scene on her ancient

TV set next to a life-sized Slavic
dummy dressed in red & black
a medallion on his tux lapel

& silver goblets on his serving tray
her trained ivy growing up the walls
& across the ceiling as she finishes with

the thinning shears never bothering to
comb just brushes neck & shoulders
then asks too late is this all right

A Grackle's-Eye View of Lakeline Mall

with his paired black pupils
set in irises yellow as a
prospector's gold he glares about

& struts his stuff with his ebony
feathers out of kilter his head thrown
back his beak pointed to a summer sky

oblivious to teenage daughters
unhappy with a mother failed to buy
the latest fad unfazed by plastic bags

filled with designer jeans only drawn
to bugs stuck on shiny grills
as he sashays in among the parking lot's

newest models then hops onto an
island with its single tree the one
will soon release a whistling chatter

when his prolific kind returns to roost
their white droppings casting
a fetid shadow as they

splat windows & roofs
while shoppers long after dark
search still for El Dorado

After Álvaro Oyarzún's *El autodidacta*

learning the art is an art
the artist first must learn
submit to being branded mad
the lowest kind of copycat

to cut up sacred comic books
& tear off a monarch's wings
to discover nature's deep design
even if it kills the colorful flight

to memorize every painful sight
through his/her subjective eyes
to mix media with encyclopedia
& slash the precious canvas alive

to accept the least accepted line
to sketch the ungainly in the nude
to reject a past day's saving grace
to create the figure few will face

to satisfy the urge to picture rage
to paint a blank will capture the age
when none will care & simply curse
criticize for being in or out of style

must go it alone & make the rules
scorned by all the leading schools
any lesson worthless until unlearned
unless self-taught the art's unearned

On Visiting NYC

become just another
autumn leaf covers
pavement instead of

earth one more
flake upon the
piles of snow

each a pattern
all its own
till sun's thaw

turns the sodden
leaves to a
soggy mass &

melting sweeps the
huddled decay into
the East River

shimmers beneath Brooklyn's
harp-like Bridge on
which Hart limned

lines forever linked
to tuned cables
still lift cabbies'

nightly fares crossing
over as did
the ferry the

current hastened with
Walt's well-joined disparate
crowds while now

descending jets with
their wing tips
blinking warning lights

wink as myriad
stars at the
city avenues lit

with welcome &
runways too at
LaGuardia & JFK

as Liberty's torch
still brightly shines
to her multitudinous

poor in sight
of Shea where
immigrants play for

exorbitant pay as
oil sheiks in
flowing robes pass

through Customs beside
bearded kippahed Zionists
with prayer shawls

fringed each so
eager to turn
his laptop on

a movie crew
from the down-under
land of koala

& kangaroo here
perhaps to reshoot

Mighty Joe Young's

attempted escape from
this asphalt cage
to climb again

the Empire State's
injection needle the
plane's fuselage decal

reading "Bombardier" resets
London aflame from
incendiaries from Luftwaffe

bays then over
Dresden's flak-filled skies
the getting even

as here Twin
Towers missing from
those prefer to

die for an
evanescent heaven than
live for the

sacred real till
fearful now which
place or edifice

next in line
o not you
Grand Central Station

your hopeful throngs
meeting trains with
open arms or

bidding fond farewells
o not you
dear Central Park

with your scads
of skaters &
your lone unheard-of

jazzer with his
familiar tones &
empty saxophone case

awaiting strangers' hands
may drop no
bomb but bill

or coin near
ponds with geese
preen on solid

rock holds up
skyscrapers & subway
riders just arrived

natives rarely leaving
belonging forming as
poets have written

a part of
your famed Indian
Dutch anonymous scene

Rondo for Mahler

Musical & Literary Mementos

for his planned "noble & charitable"
dental museum the self-styled
"Freedom Undertaker" Ondrej Jajcaj
pulled out with his pair of pliers

the rubber & porcelain prostheses
of the 19th-century's Johannes Brahms
the Czech grave-robber complimentary of
the Romantic's high-quality dentures

another case of the "attentive disease"
morbid exaggerated contemplation of
the most ordinary objects of the universe
suffered in Poe's short story by his narrator

extracts a ghastly ivory spectrum
from the pale prematurely buried gums
of Berenice his young & not long since
lovely vivacious epileptic cousin

her relatives unaware it wasn't death
referred to in Vienna as tram 71
had hurried her to the cemetery where
they laid her alive to eternal rest

the bearded composer interred at 64
yet none since then has ever removed
any root molar crown or wisdom from
the body of his solo & symphonic works

with timpani-heart opening of his First
still pumping strong & the Second's
trumpet French horn & trombone calls
triumphant still as all his vein-refrains

pulse with melodic contrapuntal strains
bite their darker tones deep in the mind
by strings & drums woodwinds & brass
blown & tongued between lips & teeth

Boat House Grill

on Friday nights
it features "Yo
Gadjo" Slim Richey's

trio at its
family-style gravel-floored venue
with two holes

in its corrugated
roof live oaks
grow up through

while from its
ceiling hangs an
entire canoe &

near it a
fake netted trout
a taxidermic real

on the entrance
wall & on
its north a

trophy next to
oars & life
preservers with outdoor

motors leaning along
a facing wooden
ledge beside a

stage of planks
barely raised with
on it amps

mikes & the
instruments already tuned
for couples below

on green picnic
benches who have
come to eat

to Western Swing
the food as
ever catfish burgers

& fries &
corn dogs for
all the kids

for the grown-ups
young & old
bock Shiner beers

sipped as now
Django Porter in
his black-&-gray toboggan

begins to twang
Reinhardt's "Swing 42"
his Gypsy namesake's

Hot Club piece
from World War
Two in tandem

with his leader
who's all decked
out in blue-jean

pants Hawaiian shirt

black white-banded hat
matching two-toned shoes

his white wispy
beard reaching not
quite down to

his palm-treed shirt
as he strums
chords & peers

at the shaking
heads through his
glitter-rimmed woman's glasses

& now on
all five strings
he rings out

"It Don't Mean
a Thing If
It Ain't Got

That Swing" &
follows it with
"There Will Never

Be Another You"
as Francie Meaux
Jeaux his barefoot

wife keeps the
beat on upright
bass while letting

out a jubilant
yell as the
clientele pat their

feet on pebbles
from creek bottom
or stream-fed lake

their children breaking
into delighted dance
& then with

the grateful tips
their parents have
sent they drop

them into the
minnow bucket of
this fisherman's dream

Community Music Fest

: New Orleans Jazz Band

their retiree quintet at this
third annual Austin event
brings alive a city missed
even by those have never

witnessed its Fat Tuesday
or its French Quarter café
whose name gave birth to
"Tin Roof Blues" their re-

vivaled version not their best
since short tonight their clari-
netist busy with a real-estate
deal but still notes blown &

banjoed render a tradition known
'round the globe heard here now
as they all come marching in to
"That's a Plenty" a barn burner

features the cornetist who started
on his horn at the 6th-grade center
later joined IBM his embouchure
in boyish shape as he rips rings &

hits high C right on the money
as did before him legendary Bix
more for love of it than any tips
the trombonist too with his instru-

ment a valve-slide combination
for other gigs wails on his mean
bass trumpet a Bach Stradivarius

the same brand as Cy Touff blew

in Herman's 1950s' Herd & with
Richie Kamuca on his tenor sax
in that West Coast style of jazz
but can tell this is Dixieland by

the old guy's washboard-cowbell-
cymbal all rolled into one his feet
dancing as fingers drive the beat
while the tuba player with on his

shoulder his helicon "the hell you
say" pumps away as in those slow
parades to the Crescent City grave
on the way back swinging out with

"O Didn't He Fly" the ghost flown
to join as mourners then believed &
some still do a heavenly host'll sing
as Louie did when soul comes home

: *Austin Civic Wind Ensemble*

from under spreading live-oak trees
listeners to set sail soon for overseas
though none need leave this Central
Market's outdoor deck for one & all

to tour by composer scores sights far
from store 18 at 38th & North Lamar
traveling through Grainger Irish reels
& the Ottorino Respighi chariot spills

P.D.Q. Bach's pixy woodland sprites
some may skip to slip inside for food
not those connoisseurs with appetites

for Dmitri Kabalevsky's Robin Hood

at their picnic tables each family eats
as musicians locate their section seats
tuning instruments before the director
lifts his hands for *Molly on the Shore*

when the woods brass & tympani stir
harbor air or cliffs & peaks of County
Cork or fuchsias & castles of Munster
coastal Kerry Carrountouhill Killarney

a patron after buying beer rushes back
on hearing trumpets stationed on stairs
behind retail shops begin their fanfares
signal now the uncaged lions' attack

of martyr-gladiators selected to fight
in Circus Maximus & to win the right
to face tomorrow another rowdy fickle
crowd at a supine Emperor's spectacle

this *Feste Romane* an orchestrated race
with drivers' whips lashing rivals' eyes
as wheels & axles roll over arms & legs
crushed to the quarter-of-a-million cries

curses hurled from a three-story height
against Blue or Green or Red or White
racers' colors barely viewed by women
sit rather & flirt with their raucous men

Ovid observing then the same old news
of another dictatorial age's dozen gates
spring wide on three-mile runs as Blues
more dejected when their favorite fades

Whites hysterical once their hero grabs

the lead when the jockeying charioteers
pass metal dolphins mark the seven laps
rounding spina posts to fanatical cheers

Virgil's epic reporting how sailor oars
power prows furrow sea shower spray
here horses foaming as teams lift roars
in waves when one gains or falls away

fans frenzied from their color's defeat
instead of seeking a better fairer order
by competing for the open Senate seat
erecting viaducts dismantling a border

these taking pleasure in historic strains
heard through pages the bandsmen turn
replaying the deadly games & the reins
let loose whose lessons are still to learn

: Oliver Rajamani & His Company

in his white silk shirt with its collar
covered by strands of jet black hair
he intently tunes his rubab's strings
tightens or loosens its wooden pegs

the fringed colored straps dangling
from a bluish tile of its fingerboard
as his tones already begin to evoke
raga vadi Pallavi & the Vedic texts

droning the power of monsoon rains
wash away & drown or heal disease
as the Ganges has for myriads bathe
in the sewage of their sacred stream

his notes echoing faintly of Tanjore

Taj Mahal untouchables suttee pyres
elephants cows caves Bengal's tigers
Tamil Kamasutra Raj Gandhi Tagore

till now he opens & is slowly joined
by the Brazilian with long thin braids
pulled out the back of his gimme cap
as he taps upon his Peruvian cajón &

his eyes peer from a deep-black face
the balding & gray-haired violinist in
a blue-jean work shirt bows as conga
player his eyes closed ring in one ear

slaps his drum & cellist with twisted
hair tied in a knot on top of his head
plucks repeating the hypnotic phrase
spellbinding those have come to hear

to be transported to that exotic place
all clapping to rhythms pounded out
on skin or strings by palm or fingers
the leader chanting unknown words

tororó habibi yah foreign but full
of urgent appeal to god or woman
or whatever mysterious force it is
may bring relief or love or release

felt by each now's drawn to dance
young & old suddenly lifting limbs
swaying hands & arms legs & hips
barefooted upon the planks of wood

a girl in red-tip cowboy boots whirls
as dress strap slips from her shoulder
& another twirls while on one of hers
a white cockatoo rides flapping wings

kiddies in tennies flip-flops & sandals
a lady wearing her wedged high heels
irresistible to all is the incantatory pull
of their blood now pulses irrepressibly

to these songs' sensual-spiritual blends
ancient call from India's endless source
a river of unseen music will ever course
to the soul's need for sound can cleanse

Jazz by the Boulevard
for Donna Van Ness

yesterday
on a temporary
outdoor stage
the Heritage
named
for the Park Cities Bank
in recognition of & to honor
this festival's money-lending sponsor
Marchel Ivery performed at 69
& today on the Coors Light Main
David "Fathead" Newman at 74
is holding forth
Marchel having honked & swung on
"Star Eyes" "Bag's Groove" & "Lover Man"
now David does the same in & on "Hard Times"
& also Hoagy's "Georgia on My Mind"
having opened with "Billie's Bounce"
as whites blacks yellows & browns of Cowtown's
crowd mill around or in portable seats
shake heads & tap their feet to the quartet's driving beat
beyond the shadow of Will Rogers' Memorial Coliseum
across from the Kimbell Art Museum
here for this "cowboy & culture" promotional scheme
a city manager's dream
to celebrate the Lone Star's native sons
to generate a few jobs & a bit of income
for local citizens most in shorts
& the majority sports
a pair of shades from the sun's late September blaze
as even in these autumn days
it just keeps burning on
bright & unseasonably strong
with a little of the force

of these Texas tenors
blowing yet with might & main
despite age's unrelenting aches & pains
rhythm-a-ning or improvising a blues
or on pop tunes of Tin Pan Jews
bringing joy to all have come to hear
who never knew a Ku Klux fear
here one block over from Camp Bowie
the brick-paved street intersects University
where the admission is gratis
thanks to Cadillac's
major financial grant & to volunteers
manning booths include that Rocky Mountain beer's
causes one to wonder does hurt & happiness accord
with the roots of a minor chord
can the melodic blend in any song
set right a lingering wrong
seems so to go by the loving-it look
when these Black men cook
with their hard-bop licks
their soulful stratospherics
a look apparent on every listener's face
regardless of race
or place of birth
due in part to an elegant auto's corporate worth
but more to elder statesmen hanging on
to produce a dateless priceless tone

Rondo for Mahler

one hundred years
from the time
he penned his

Ninth one hundred
five from the
date of his

Sixth have tried
to imagine him
coming back though

in spite of
Gospels & Hamlet's
ghost whoever has

yet wonder what
he would have
made of compact

discs render his
nine & unfinished
Tenth his own

versions will never
hear except for
recordings with him

performing a pianola
transcription of his
Fourth's finale &

from his Fifth
its first movement's
four-note fateful knock

Beethoven's famed tattoo
Gustav changed to
the one same

trumpet pitch until
with the second
time it returns

instead of down
the phrase's final
note goes gloriously

up & so
depend for his
orchestral sound on

conductors such as
Mengelberg who knew
him then whom

W.C. Williams in
his *In the
American Grain* likens

to mother Lincoln
in beard top
hat & woman's

shawl hovering over
his nation torn
by Civil War

coaxing from aching
instruments tumultuous loads
though Willem's Adagietto's

too saccharine perhaps

for the redemption
its composer meant

by his manic
transcendent theme how
many stars would

that maestro now
receive from Amazon
reviewers who rate

the latest CDs
with Gustav understudy
Bruno Walter's "Resurrection"

& Claudio Abbado's
Seventh earning five
though Sony has

yet to reissue
the former's wondrous
Ninth to bring

back from '55
Eduard Flipse's Rotterdam
Sixth maybe out

of print because
Mitchell graded it
"aspiring but mediocre"

o how it
hurt to read
of that critic's

cutting critique of
the very LP
on which first

heard his Andante
with its ardent
Alma 6th her

interval a "longing
languishing leap" followed
by its anguishing

minor turn captures
her though considered
by some "more

sob than song"
those assert it
disturbs & makes

trivial the classical
form others so
certain he took

no pleasure in
its torturous melodic
line & yet

when he played
it for her
they wept together

his cantabile love
in returning again
has moved to

this centennial review
of the notices
& unkind cuts

include those accuse

Bernstein of directing
overindulgent emotional shows

when he it
was in part
recovered the symphonist's

art with the
Reich defeated &
ovens opened though

prior to Holocaust
Gustav gone &
yet had known

Wagner's Aryan supermen
before invention of
phonograph & film

could have saved
Gustav's grail baton
replayed his magic

wand in conducting
his Seventh with
its sentimental its

ironic parodic tangle
of lugubrious ländler
& misty cow-belled

nocturne how to
tell which recordings
to choose of

which he would
have approved with
Simon Rattle's Tenth

only given 3½
the Third of
Jesús López-Cobos &

James Conlon's Fifth
awarded 5 the
same for Fritz

Reiner's definitive Fourth
& can Olson's
Black Mountain Projectivism

light the trail
through cold hell
& selva oscura

as do the
winds & strings
through "harmonic thicket"

"to pastoral tone"
or is it
all "a dreadful

farce" as Christensen
stated predating Hopkins'
essay in the

Barham *Perspectives* volume
his piece on
form in the

turning-point Fifth opens
with its "torment
of uncertainty" its

"becoming" requires "one

perception lead quickly
to the next

until all are
exhausted" & true
as well for

listener & conductor
as Mitchell declares
(with likely Flipse's

Sixth in mind):
"to survive the
length of the

symphony's finale alone
one needs a
musical constitution of

almost unnatural strength"
& goes too
for working one's

way through Jonathan
Williams's *Jubilant Thicket*
with its poem

on each symphonic
section which for
the Third's 2nd

movement draws upon
its "What the
Flowers in the

Meadow Tell Me"
selecting naturally for
the Fifth's rondo

a nature thought
from Thoreau's June
journal from Schoenberg

how he got
more out of
watching Gustav knot

his tie than
bigwigs treating sacred
subjects & were

Gustav to return
would he be
even half-surprised to

learn Ives (who
in one Jonathan
limerick gives hives

to those hear
his recycled hymns)
with more than

one CD for
each of that
Connecticut Yankee's symphonies

since had the
Austrian lived had
planned to conduct

Charles's Third anointed
him America's greatest
composer carried its

score home with

him to his
early death in

his land struggled
to come to
terms with his

expressive Bohemian mode
those sort of
Mitchell's words in

Walter's "Vienna a
musical battlefield" where
citizens fought over

art with an
impassioned partisanship while
Gustav's own tempestuous

temperament loosed storms
about his head
fisticuffs at the

first performance of
his innocent Fourth
his excesses still

in '57 arousing
hostile reviews &
yet he knew

his time would
come & by
'60 catalogs offering

5 competing readings
of First 2
of Second 3

of Fourth &
2 of the
Ninth the Sixth

with a single
disc the Flipse
"aspiring but mediocre"

inspiring nonetheless as
is Abaddo's of
the Seventh's strains

"native to the
night" even if
an ear-trained friend

knows far more
judged the whole
"a big disjointed

bunch of episodes
the Finale just
will never work"

the same magnificent
soaring rondo how
ever be brought

to agree can
any two yet
do with Mitchell's

nothing kills his
music like the
cozy approach smoothing

over soft-pedaling rather

than exposing his
noisy march thumb-to-nose

will ever accept
his intractable uncivil
double-faced moods his

nocturnes recurring not
trite but fighting
to unfold with

"unnatural strength" with
linked dynamic extremes
guide one Virgil-like

through brambles dense
with conflicting chords
in himself &

in affinitive souls
as he waltzes
all through darkest

woods of macabre
scherzos to the
adagios of luminous

pulse wring the
heart with a
delicious pain would

endure again &
again a suffering
never repeated enough

Presidential Doggerel

Presidential Doggerel

FDR

the day he died
they drafted Dad
the war still on
which he declared

in his famous speech
on that sneak attack
but if heard it then
could not understand

since December '41
just turned 2 & a ½
& if caught on radio
his fireside chats

it would have been
with Uncle Alvin
but mostly listened
to squeaking doors

the sinister laughter
of the Inner Sanctum
unaware that Mom &
Dad had voted for him

wonder what they thought
of WPA & his First Lady
kept company with Blacks
if they knew in California

of internment camps
Warm Springs in Georgia
his visits to its waters

for his polio legs

at Yalta wrapped in a blanket
awaiting iron curtain of death
while he Churchill & Stalin
divided East from West

Republicans propose
to remove his image
from Mint's thin dime
& to replace it with

the Gipper's face
claiming Reagan alone
brought with Berlin's Wall
Communism down

too young to recall
the Second World War
depend upon a replay
of newsreel footage

where see his mole
& hear his rolling
reassuring voice
reminds of New Deal art

its Depression photos
the folk music saved
the murals painted
on Post Office walls

Truman

on Aunt Sis's carpet
we cousins all played
with pick-up sticks

built houses of cards

& by then could read
the newspaper reports
of the count in Korea
of MIGs shot down

from then remember
first feeling anger
at his having demoted
General MacArthur

on his crossing of
the demilitarized zone
only years later would find
Harry had formed a part

of the Kansas City machine
bootlegged in Prohibition
its nightlife attracted & hired
many a Texas jazz musician

"Hot Lips" Budd & Buster
blues men & women too
with their chorded notes
made up for a broken law

in '45 first learned letters
& words on Dick & Jane
not yet of buck-stops-here
or a lonely decision made

to mushroom human skin
but later perhaps to read
when the front page said
he'd not been re-elected

in bold mistaken headline

before the counting done
morning edition declaring
Thomas Dewey had won

once caught from early TV
his daughter Margaret sing
maybe at Constitution Hall
her smiling poppa beaming

light off of glasses gleaming
with he himself at the piano
his tough talk if as blinding
still strong right or wrong

Eisenhower

in hindsight obvious now
witch hunts under him
ruined many a reputation
& even whole careers

knew by then Mom & Dad's
dislike for Adlai Stevenson
& only in those elections
both had voted Republican

still picture likable Ike
playing a round of golf
once he'd won the War
added to highway system

where Beatniks had a ball
driving cross-country in
their open-road rebellion
against rampant consumerism

& give him credit

for his standing firm
after he had sent in
to Little Rock High

the National Guard
to escort those students
took the first brave steps
up steep Integration stairs

& for selecting the flag
of Bob Heft's design
his school assignment
received a low-B grade

till Dwight found it best
& has since '60 served
as old red white & blue
of 50 stars & 13 stripes

JFK

can never forget
that day in Dallas
ashamed as a Texan
& yet forever proud

had voted for him at 21
a Catholic of Irish descent
whose Ask Not speech
inspired a generation

his Peace Corps youth
so eager to serve abroad
his support of microchip
put two men on the moon

in the Cuban missile crisis

by calling up the Reserves
he'd take the Russians on
& even back them down

only later to recognize
he had quoted the final line
from Milton's Italian sonnet
on those only stand & wait

can hope had he survived
he would've ended sooner
as some say he would have
that fiasco in Vietnam

LBJ

at first had regretted
he inherited the job
but glad when he signed
the Civil Rights Act

yet lament he listened
to Pentagon's advice
such a tragic figure
in his closing years

but with pride & pleasure
visit on UT's campus
the library-museum bears
his initialed name

where hear him tell
in his recorded
hill-country drawl
the tale of a man

on growing deaf

informed his doctor
who told him straight
he must give up the bottle

but the patient replied
he preferred his drink
to most anything
he had ever heard

Nixon

remain conflicted by
the debt have ever owed
to the exchange program
he helped to start

after going to Caracas
as Veep to Ike
where protestors stoned his car
where it made him think

the States should send
young college students south
to dialogue with Latin nations
led to that Chilean trip

to my wedded Beauty
nearly everything else
he did or stood for
could never stand

the arrogance of Agnew
& the bugging plumbers
those Watergate tricks
can never forgive

yet can't but feel

half sorry to see
from the helicopter door
his two-fingered Vs

before the two flew off
though more for Pat
his faithful wife
who stood at his side

right to the bitter end
even believe in a way
our marriage makes up
for all his own mistakes

Ford

a dullard it seemed
& mostly just recall
the position he played:
center in Michigan ball

hiking to quarterbacks
more accurate & quick
then making the blocks
on the rushing defense

in the middle of games
though given no chance
to carry across the line
into an end-zone glory

but then with his pardon
of Dick he helped to heal
festering national wound
& made the guilt official

Carter

a Bible-toting peanut farmer
Shakespeare-quoting Navy man
Georgia governor Southern poet
in the White House said to be

way out of his depth
too decent or just naïve
done in by the Iranians
a wheat deal with Russians

& despite Camp David Accord
& all the classic books
he & Rosalyn read together
was denied a second term

defeated by a B-rated star
& yet would find years later
another & maybe truer calling
as humanity's habitat hammer

Reagan

the great cowlick communicator
a caricature asleep at the wheel
with blow-dry & make-up mask
bonzo at bedtime in Oval Office

but his fans all applauded
his command performance
on firing air-controllers
smuggling Contras arms

approving even in uniform
the perjury of Colonel North
Conservatives still consider him

the absolute best of their kind

none before or since
can half compare
but for all he did
don't give a flip

wouldn't pay to see
any part he ever played
from unconvincing cowboy
to State of the Union speech

Bush I

learned to read his lips
for the promises a silver-
spooned politician feeds
easily bamboozled ears

to view paid TV ads
showed the opposition
setting hardened criminals
free on American streets

& in between knew innuendo
character assassination out-
right fibs plain faux pas contra-
diction & his recommending

ketchup as a substitute for
healthy school-lunch veggies
& the list goes on & on
his wife was even worse

& yet unlike his lesser son
didn't overextend his Iraqi stay
for Father Knew Best

left Baghdad's treasures alone

Clinton

the great white hope
the only one
ever saw in person
all the others viewed

on the TV set
or the cover of *Life*
in Movietone newsreels
or *The World at War*

but too far away
to see him clearly
Al Gore either
just amplified voices

though voted for the pair
yet expected much more
than either one or the other
was ever able to deliver

since even such qualities
as youth attractive looks
& the articulate speech
can deceive & disappoint

& yet can give him points
for sending Kosovo aid
& George Mitchell to resolve
the Irish civil strife

& even for the little jazz
he'd improvise on tenor
although will ever regret

that unlit uninhaled cigar

Bush II

b-b gun & toy pistol
what boys in Texas
did not include them
on their Christmas list

even the morning
of Peace on Earth
Goodwill to Men
could hardly wait

for night to end
so hoping to find
beneath the tree
a package containing

a six shooter at least
with round paper caps
in a replica chamber
could turn & fire

as out the barrel came
puffs of smoke & life-
like sound just as in
any Western matinee

though none ever died
from popping powder
in Saturday features
with Roy or Gene

the same ugly villains
returned each week
to the silver screen

but for Dubya to pack

his captured revolver
from Saddam Hussein
how many thousands
of dead & wounded

ruined homes & lives
just so he could play
marshal of law & order
upright tough protector

with insurgents thrown
in water-boarding cells
tortured in Abu Ghraib
his weapon shown off

to White House guests
as kids on b-days exhibit
their long-awaited gifts
to neighborhood gangs

not knowing enough
as a full-grown man
to be afraid of a wish
had childishly made

Obama

his election would liken
to finding religion
even more his re-election
still brings relief

from seeing him appear
on the TV screen
in support of a law

for the health of all

what wealthy love to call
Obamacare swear everyday
they'll repeal its mandate
that each must pay

so 30 million receive
pre-condition coverage
that meek & blessed poor
not inherit political wind

while the Christian Right
not about to allow them in
to hospital or sanctuary pew
no birther believing on him

over a right to life the rich
defend the 2nd Amendment
oppose a background check
any limit on the multiple clip

& ever berate the 47 per cent
for taking the sinful hand-outs
unaccepting an unlivable wage
paid by those so piously prey

Epilogue

María will always ask
why would anyone want
to lead this country
it's such a thankless task

even if later on
a grateful history judge
a term more worthy

than it ever seemed

none for sure can say
whether or not with time
even Bushes' standings
may both improve

from here the chances
are looking slim
for anything to redeem
their dreadful years

& yet Shrub's notion
democracy will moderate
extreme religious views
in Malaysia's coming true

in other Asian places too
& have to admit he sent
Africa AIDs assistance
makes art instead of war

his name whatever the case
has been engraved & forms
part of a distinguished line
starts with another George

owned but freed his slaves
then Abe to emancipate all
& the whole nation to save
later Rough Riding Teddy

with big stick talking soft
a warm place in his heart
for Yellowstone Yosemite
& every other national park

if most erred in judgment

Jefferson's Purchase endures
explored by Lewis & Clark
many left no mark on office

some got in when better men
failed to toss a hat in the ring
a Tippecanoe swept Tyler in
blame electorate praise it too

The Cowtown Circle

The Cowtown Circle

*for/after exhibit curators
Scott Barker Jane Myers
Ronald Watson Mark L.
Smith & Stephen Pinson*

back then their art still lay ahead
but even in War was being made
though unsuspected then & only
come upon at a '92 exhibition in

the Huntington Gallery long after
had built from Uncle Alvin's Vic-
tory garden those corn-stalk forts
no defense against an Axis attack

just played like after the Saturday
matinees at the White Theater on
Hemphill Street in this city where
the West began as an outpost pro-

tecting from the real not those pic-
tured redskin raids yet even by '39
Bror Utter in a manifesto declared
bluebonnet & Indian paintbrushes

cattle auctions & rodeos all old hat
he & other Circle artists inspired in-
stead by an imported Parisian style
of abstracts myths & masquerades

in fourth grade aspired to cowboy-
Indian sketches of classmate drew
if knew Amon Carter collection of
Remington oils & Russell-sculpted

broncobusters do not recall but did
watch as bulls spilled riders at Will
Rogers Coliseum memorial to wit-
ty trick roper statued on horseback

outside in actual cactus as clowns
inside distracted till safe & sound
saw the tall-necked giraffes if not
the one by Veronica Helfensteller

sits at a table with girl & mandrill
her tea party for the social baboon
of '43 or her *Animals at the Zoo* of
'46 with it may be a baby alligator

not so gruesome as when with full-
sized frightful teeth & armored tail
one rose up from lily pads to fasci-
nate in its rock-lined pond the last

to visit Sundays when the engineer
blew the whistle on miniature train
reminds of their "intimate modern-
ism" has transformed time & place

as has her '47 *Poor Little Girl Who
Swallowed the Seeds* where two gi-
raffes look on as vines grow out of
her ears & nostrils' holes while she

pets perhaps a greyhound & a cat's
curled up beside her thin bare foot
had only been read to that story of
bean stalks climbed to giant's gold

but knew nothing then or there nor
anything anywhere like her etched
plates & yet passed on the city bus

to Downtown "Y" that St. Ignatius

still there though wouldn't have rec-
ognized the Victorian-era Academy
in her haunted lithograph *The Three
Guardians* of '43 with spooky trees

& two white foreground female fig-
ures like floating ghosts glide back
of its low black wrought-iron fence
another standing on a 3rd-floor roof

arms as if ready to fly or leap into a
stormy moonlit sky or onto the leaf-
strewn ground below or into cedars
can only make out two of those jig-

saw-puzzled creatures in her *Three
Virgins Three Giraffes & Turtle* of
'45 facing opposite ways as a hat-
less virgin turns exchanging looks

with on her right one tallest living
quadruped the other virgins sport-
ing feathered hats staring straight
ahead at three pears on table one

per plate while the turtle stretches
its neck to peer up from the beach
or bank at pair of pears on another
plate & beside it a bunch of grapes

her alter-ego also featured in '47's
The House that Jack Built alone in-
side with a single bird flies outside
no dog cat rat cock horse cow as in

Mother Goose accumulative rhyme

all the prints small from a war-time
shortage of metal & paper Dad giv-
ing up on his Standard Printing Co.

at 1404 Throckmorton as big outfits
kept him from even a limited supply
then taken on for Vultee night shifts
riveting B-24 Flying Coffins & part-

time at elder Utter's lithograph firm
his son in rinsing with collodion the
large glass plates & learning a trade
later to produce an "unrealistic love-

liness" Bror's '41 *Lady With a Box*
he & confreres inhabiting a parallel
space as in '46's *Garden of Earthly
Delights* one teems with serpentine

3-fingered & pastel-tinctured forms
Evening Reflections of '49 with sets
of pinchers holding round or oblong
half-sliced shapes in divided shades

in *The Dreamer* of '46 a nude sleeps
recumbent on the striated surface of
cut stone slab or trunk as curvaceous
as she alongside one with a blue-line

drawing of a man down on one knee
lifts his arms as if were calling upon
some power above though atop that
rock-like altar two snails just inch a-

long while elsewhere a frog pelican
& another man's head all imprinted
as on mushrooms growing from rot-
ten wood whose meaning is as hard

to come by as the four-leaf clover in
Granny's yard with its vitex tempted
to the forbidden climb after a May St.
Eve with her olive skin's unforgotten

his '45 *Tree of Knowledge* revealing
rather than rings two nude lovers em-
bracing & a female trio dances naked
plus four fish bird leaf & flower vase

from '45 too a *Woman Combing Her
Hair* where on a table an oval mirror
reflects her face beside an amputated
foot a hand heads & six fowl observ-

ing as chickens beneath peck in grass
all as little understood as his untitled
pieces with not so living appendages
flags in '53 *Signals* can signify more

held by men wear variegated tights in
arched niches a similar architectonics
in his '52 *Pharmaceutical Cabinet II*
each vial & bottle with shelf to itself

& before it in his '45 *Cells* men push
against a wall or ceiling as undressed
woman lies with her legs spread wide
in compartments a fish pitcher & crab

his *Cloisters* from '48 stacked arched
openings within them a figure apiece
ballet dancers male & female a kneel-
ing nude a hatted lady's fully clothed

in '60 *Fortress* chess-like pieces on-
ly one a man head-to-foot each parti-
tioned off as vessels too cubicled on

rectangular shelves in his '52 *Nun's*

Distillery as if each man woman animate thing an island after all a lonely pigeon-holed being but if artist focus on isolate life does comparison apply

have identified more with a '67 view of university under construction then Bror's *New Buildings and Pyramid— Cholula* knew it in '75 teaching there

at the foot of its pile a cathedral surmounts & a blue-pink Mexican sky he reticulated in his painting whereas undrafted in War etched intaglio

prints the '41 or '43 *Man in the Pit* with a surreal dream-like "creatcher" sits perhaps on Bror's right shoulder '44's soft-ground biomorphic *Strata*

with its "unseen world" manipulated by a breathing it in more deeply even than this native place a shared habitat were born to though different to each

not known nor remembered the same given facts to leave or take without or with them to create in a simultaneous or another time verities of each's own

Cacti from '45 would seem the closest he'd come to a flora or fauna of a local kind & so changed had to read its label for perceiving the nopal & prickly pear

Mexican Lia Cuilty's '43 untitled nude

brings Daphne to life on turning her in-
to a desertic tree & in '44 she'd depict
the family ranch in *The Day's at Morn*

regionalism after Thomas Hart Benton
with its fertile fields & a flock of geese
as white as their house & all their trees
filled with leaves not bare as Daphne's

but believe it less than Cynthia Brants'
'45 *Horse and Rider* though only sat at
four on a Shetland pony for a '43 photo
in a vest & pair of chaps Granny sewed

yet rather prefer the '37 *Trotting Horse*
her color aquatint with lines of legs sug-
gest the animal in movement printed on
paper & admire her later photogravures

like '83's *Shades of Times Past* origami
its men with weapons on running steeds
out of folded sheets as too her *Trooper's
Horse* of '82 though that bronzed paper

unlike Bror she would both saddle up
& craft her equines to gallop & capri-
ole to leaps & hind-leg kicks till a rid-
ing accident left her with broken back

& in a plaster cast decorated by Circle
friends who made of her a work of art
while her "elaborate bawdy jokes" re-
galed all & with spirit untamed as any

unbreakable mare competed as jumper
whose slightest shift of hand weight or
leg her show horse responsive to on ex-
ecuting maneuvers intricate as her ardu-

ous process with copper plates as in her
Yesterday's Paper of '69 with its ad for
a Mobile Homes' gigantic sale wadded
up & in seventeen steps that image pre-

pared with gelatin film photo emulsion
contact exposed to the positive desired
made from a negative bathed diluted &
dissolved in acid at varied density rates

her medium well-known from portraits
by Curtis of his proud aborigine chiefs
among her '69 subjects *Low Light on a
Beach & Momentous* landing on moon

that shot had taken from a TV screen
& now *A Golf Swing* of '93 recalling
those sand traps at Colonial's course
laid out alongside the Trinity banks

though never caddied on its private
fairways never played on bentgrass
after driving nine or eighteen holes
just putted eastside's public greens

yet allows for feel of a Titleist ball
she hit with her aquatint color arcs
as if by a Ben Hogan wood or iron
his arms & body following through

in '41 Kelly Fearing had in explor-
ing an attic found a shadeless lamp
its nude torso missing porcelain el-
bow to armpit the wires once held

he too reproducing an old newspa-
per but this on canvas black white
& gray with headline upside down

Germa[ny] attacks Russians Japan

invades again two ties drape above
from coat hanger instead of a neck
with lives ending or interrupted by
cruel racist world gone power mad

but before the *Attic Piece* had done
in birth year his '39's *Jitterbuggers*
with its girls' swinging skirts show-
ing their knees & a red panty of one

such dances Mom & Dad had saved
up for awaited each week to drive to
or ride with friends & hear big bands
out at Lake Worth his favorite Duke

at times would just stand next to him
& watch as pianist with drums guitar
& bass would hit together on *Merry-
Go-Round* also on *Rockin' in Rhythm*

but partial too to Jimmie's *Lunceford
Special* with its high trumpet work &
stirring trombone of Trummy Young
Joe Thomas with that booming tenor

never said if Harry James a member
of the first band its Casino Ballroom
hired when George Smith the owner
objected to that future trumpet star's

blasting with gusto & had its leader
seat him back behind the other men
but paid him quite a sum in years to
come for that golden horn out front

no need to say they would not have

gone on East Rosedale for listening
to an Ornette Coleman brand of Be-
bop much less his Harmolodic licks

yet neither to express any prejudice
like most from their Depression age
just didn't care for the '40s' sounds
a New Generation had begun to dig

now wonder did they ever go & see
the Circle innovations on display in
a gallery of their city library before
its move from Throckmorton & 9th

& if saw them there had they said a
thing if they did don't retain a word
no image at all since surely to them
a universe as of verse were never so

curious to know not a poem nor Lia
Cuilty's *The Grapevine Swing* a fun
had later on if not by '45 when won
3rd place for her little redheaded girl

canopied by dead austere trees cer-
tainly not *Arrested Flight* from '43
with its pink square-topped triangu-
lar-footed cones & blue antennaed

moth no such art to appeal to them
nor clowns to entertain in Dickson
Reeder's *The Dispute* of '44 since
a pair out of its trio glares in anger

Kelly's *The Kite Flyers* might have
caught my eye if in '45 at six knew
how to fly but its sinister white obe-
lisks & constructs shaped as A & U

must have just put off if still unable
to read its other world lies behind &
if that anger in a comedic scene un-
sensed how a black in overalls pull-

ing a white child's happiness string
while looking as fearful as she from
an unseen menace can feel in atmo-
sphere more than in clouds or wind

as for the group's Halloween soiree
in painting by Emily Guthrie Smith
it may've seemed oddly funny with
bearded man in casket wholly alive

extending one hand to a lady in her
long red dress as the hooded monk
eyes hidden by mask & other hand
held in palms administers last rites

& tube-headed figure in light-blue
cut-off nightie with a fan at drawn
red lip points finger at living dead
as black-face mammy Hallelujahs

Veronica's own version of scene
in her '43 *The Host in the Coffin*
has tube-head too but wears blue-
&-red tights & touches hands of

Dickson in his & Flora's home at
2411 6th Avenue where party took
place blocks from Granny's three
May St. houses one Dad rented at

3019 lower middle-class address
no mansion as on Elizabeth Bou-
levard intersects with the avenue

yet memories' & poetry's source

though only suppose it was there
the Reeders had invited all those
who shared such artwork as *Host*
with its lit candelabra its guest in

leotards stands on white laced-up
roller skates by one in Hindu sari
while a male at the foot of a stair
ignoring death takes a ballet step

Reading the Cards a Flora Blanc
of '43 she a New Yorker Chaïm
Soutine model studied with Fer-
nand Léger met Dickson in Paris

working at Atelier of printmaker
Stanley Hayter & married in '37
when moving to Dickson's birth-
place introduced the avant-garde

in '46 rather than making her art
Flora training children to act in a
performance of Thackeray's *The
Rose & the Ring* & in '48 putting

on *A Midsummer Night's Dream*
Oberon's metallic costume Dick-
son designed & painted as he had
the sets for their Makepeace play

he working mostly as a portraitist
of often his Circle friends the best
similarity he'd catch may've been
of the cerebral-palsied Bill Bomar

right fist resting against his cheek

below square eyeglasses the other
hand with fingers cupping his ear
a frame to lips mustache & beard

caught above all his fellow artist's
peering eyes intent through lenses
his affliction here under control as
when in contact with brush or pen

at touch of paper turned oil or ink
into blue jay's pool as in that '44
painting with its bird beside half-
circles shimmering & frogs swim-

ming if fish differ from Fearing's
float in his see-through aquarium
while here rippling waters spread
to lily pad with star-white flower

as then in Granny's double pond
she'd clean in summer when out
on freshly-sanded bottoms cous-
ins would wade & duck beneath

its pools cooled till the lilies hy-
acinths moss & goldfish brought
from washtubs back within palo-
pinto-rocked rims & steps across

yet Bill skilled too in portraiture
as instance cite a '44 likeness of
Dickson's big dark eyes & reced-
ing hairline mirrored by his curv-

ing collar though favor from '42
his *Santa Fe View* can fulfill a re-
gional need for landscape near &
dear's chamisa & Apache plume

but if those appear in the picture
must study more closely its dots
& crosshatching to rediscover in
& by his art other familiar sights

Baird

The Book's East-Texas Tour
for Bill & Ann Faulkner

a copy sent to friends
husband & wife of 51 years
retired on Callender Lake

in their gracious home
with on its walls
his photos framed

one of a blue crane
another of moonlight off the water
glowing through the pines

& the sweet-gum leaves
still romantic as is
their life together

at their address where
by media mail
with the aid of workers

male & female
it will hopefully soon arrive
through the P.O. in Murchison

population 592
as of 2000 census
fifteen days it's been en route

with stops along the way
in larger & smaller
towns & cities

went first by air from Austin
to the Big D sorting station
& from there can see

on the computer screen
by the on-line record
of its tracking number

its odyssey then begins
not in Ithaca but Athens
home to Trinity Valley

Community College
& the "Black-Eyed Pea
Capital of the World"

for every place has
or ought to have
its claim to fame

but remembered more
for other friends
a teacher here of Homer

& his wife gives piano lessons
had Cicero with her
in a Latin class

she a kind of Circe
who turns rowdy kids into
tamed lovers of delicate sounds

from here going on to Sacul
with its 170 inhabitants
whose Bluegrass Opry's held

the 4th Saturday of every month
featuring performances by
old-time country & gospel bands

its namesake Lucas Collins
based on his first
spelled in reverse

since elsewhere in the State
taken by another town
the case as well with Reklaw

the next spot the volume saw
if one can say a book can see
without the miraculous eyes

for reading words
can paint a scene
their writer may have seen

its blind letters a sight
can open up the mind
to any image or thought

its name too backwards
after Margaret Walker's last
she who donated the land

for its site straddles
Rusk & Cherokee counties
with subtropical humid climate

2.3 miles southeast
on Highway 2 0 4
Flying M Ranch

holds its Annual Fly-In
where over 500 planes
come for October autumns

the pilots pitching tents
camping & kicking back
but having to land & take off

at their own risk
since its 4000 ft. grassy runway
unapproved by FAA

then continuing on to Coppell
a 30,000 + bedroom suburb
once a village with farms

settled by German & French
"Gibbs Station" before renamed
for an English railway financier

among its native sons
a famous Jason
but not of the Golden Fleece

this with his sir name Witten
Pro Bowl Cowboys tight end
on that Dallas football team

then back again to Sacul
& wonder whether
it found return worthwhile

how ever judge if haven't been
since the attraction may remain
even for where one happily left

then back & forth
from Sacul to Coppell
until going on to Tyler

"Rose Capital of the World"
birthplace too of another jock
a Cyclops of a fullback

though ever so sweet a guy
his nickname Tyler Rose
but also Earl the Pearl

as if a *Beowulf* pigskin hero
an eponymous Campbell soup
whose stiff-arm was umm-umm good

then heading back to Dallas
after perhaps some clerk decided
they needed to start from scratch

as some in life would like to do
though others would just repeat
or maybe change a thing or two

but do it over & enjoy it more
could be its tracks
retraced because

the zip code written wrong
although if that was so
has turned out right for this song

from its revisiting of
a few of the places
had driven through before

but without their histories known
hopefully its paper binding
has not been bent or broken

& even though delivery's slow
if it's ever looked into
it should still mean the same

or maybe even more
from passing through so many spots
with their storied names

its well-traveled mailer
touched by those
have enabled its epic trip

Serenading the Neighbors

when younger I would leave the window open
that those might hear jazz or classical I played
not sounds of my own but records others made
hearing them certain they would love them too

if any heard none either complained or praised
in later years I would leave the window closed
even on nights without the air-conditioning on
once I could see how presumptuous I had been

& then last week I recalled that arrogant youth
when down the street a brass quintet rehearsed
within the leader's garage with the door left up
the whole block having to hear the instruments

whether we wanted to or not but o I did indeed
walking there to be closer to the glorious notes
I watched listened & applauded for every piece
as those had not for a music I'd forced on them

Granny's Dragonflies

hovering as helicopters
above her lily
pads & blooms

they would dart
back & forth
make hair-pin turns

abruptly stop as
their multifaceted eyes
spied a mosquito

midge or fly
the nymphs beneath
the water in

larval or naiad
stage feeding on
tadpoles with extendable

jaws the adults
turning prey to
frogs spiders goldfish

lizards & birds
while the larva
as such could

survive five years
the adults lived
six months at

most their six-directional
transparent wings so
quick their stop-&-go

predatory flight hardly

visible their devil's
darning needle name

emblematic of evil
yet of courage
too a symbol

& folklore says
will stitch &
restore a wounded

snake as memory
can the long-ago
leak dried up

her double pond

María's Alstroemeria

not knowing what gift
to buy for her
to celebrate our 48th
then found this flower

with its lance-shaped leaves
& on its flare-hued
petals dash-like upright streaks
as if sparks spewed

against their orangey-yellow skies
from the harmless volcanoes
of vivid livid ovaries
& after thinking those

with Incan or Peruvian
lilies their non-Linnaean names
might for her mean
but too-bright gaudy flames

read on the label
hybrid of summer-grown Brazilian
with the winter-bred perennial
from her own thin

land north to south
of her native Chile
she has lived without
for almost now half-a-century

not knowing the length
love's fire would last
while this bouquet's one-week
guarantee has already passed

yet uprooted from the
earth in a vase
of water still lovely
as she who place

of birth did sacrifice
& her relations' lives
for mine me this
match endures & thrives

María's Ideas

at first accepted few or none
almost all rejected out of hand
& automatic would prefer my own

argued hers were too much trouble
would require money we didn't have
though really just my giving in

for always it was utterly clear
hers better & made more sense
like the faithful used VW van

she conceived we ought to buy
for its convenient side door slides
two seats for kids & pets

with one removed for hauling sand
gravel & her organic garden soil
to transport the tiles to replace

the dusty dirty carpets she felt
so harmful to all our health
& having learned the hard way

marriage math means a little expense
can make for a contented wife
I had paid the asking price

& then one day she thought
we needed a bit more space
yet liked no house she saw

so decided to add to this
& had me call for estimates
to expand out behind the back

the first the house's original cost

so had me phone another place
Erik arriving to hear her plan

for an addition above the garage
& leaning against his pickup truck
he quickly penciled a simple design

of walls with a half bath
& rooms for each of us
hers for desk & sewing machine

mine for shelves CDs & books
into hers would move a bed
for visits from family & friends

Erik's bid only half as much
his job finished right on time
& still take such pleasure in

this plot too saccharine for some
for although true as any tragedy's
hers with a genial comic outcome

Baird

after *Early Days in Callahan County* (ca. 1966)
by Brutus Clay Chrisman

Prologue

are there no more stories to tell
none comes to mind
& why is that

they used to show up on their own
or would easily call them up
but now it seems

they're done with me or I myself
have run out of things to say
& yet the world

goes right on something new every day
& the old themes are still around
& just as good as they ever were

loyalty & betrayal
art music jazz & classical
all should still inspire

but somehow they have lost their power
to move to words
as they did before

in free form or rhyming patterns
in stanzas long or short
couplets quatrains tercets cinquains

& behold the next-to-last have come again
despite a feeling they never would
the fault not theirs

nor of any thing or place
just mine alone from knowing
of all I've written

how little or nothing
can still hold up
while the others' poems

will always read
with renewed delight
Chaucer's *Troilus & Criseyde*

a Boccaccio tale from Trojan days
retold in Geoffrey's royal rime
but why repeat it

or any other
since many a plot
lies ready at hand

like the one for years
has gone on haunting
yet avoided out of fear

could not believably enter
or should not
its dark disturbing past

its history of one who
took another's life
but then as once

a college professor had said
just do it for yourself
learn a lesson or two

or none
but get it down
even if no one picks it up

or if any should
& drops it after a single line
revisit that tragic time

not to condemn or pardon
but to listen to & live with
if never to understand

Relations

soon after the century turned
Grandad moved his family here
to this railroad's shipping point
roundhouse repair shops & yard
among mesquite & prickly pear

coupling & uncoupling the cars
lifting levers for switching tracks
signaling with lantern or flag
through heat waves or northers
as bluebonnets bloomed in spring

ten years after they came
the 1905 frame station replaced
by its 1911 Prairie-style brick
with overhanging eaves' decorative belt
Flemish-like parapet & low-pitched roof

its wide horizontal architectural look
a reaction against the vertical
assembly-line mass-produced Greek & Roman
intended to appear as if
grown naturally from scrubby plain

known today for antique stores
a dozen lining Market Street
& for 1912's runaway train
caused three locomotives to collide
more than for its hanging

the County's one & only
among legally last in State
eight years later Daddy born
delivered by Dr. Robert Griggs
he with his own concoction

cured flu cases in '17
gave it over the phone
to patients free of charge
nothing Dad had spoken of
for was only two-years old

nor ever mentioned that execution
just recalled riding his mule
to the local Boy-Scouts troop
with his dime for joining
but was not let in

if aware of that event
it couldn't have been from
the newspaper headlines of 1906
on young Emma Blakely murdered
of justice done in 1907

maybe later his folks recounted
their sitting in that courtroom
listening as their neighbors testified
finding verdict & sentence just
or having perhaps their doubts

I'd only come in 2001
to find if the relatives
recorded in some centennial volume
but in courthouse's basement library
could locate not a trace

just that history unknown before
the names of those involved
in yellowed clippings on display

in a dusty see-through case
the crime & reasons why

Alberto Vargas

nothing have read has said
what had brought him here
in one letter he wrote
fate had played a role

if he arrived by boxcar
or alighted from a coach
or made it on foot
no one seemed to know

after he arrived in 1906
in late or early spring
no address is given for
where he was living then

since the letter also states
it would shock the boarders
perhaps he roomed in housing
Texas & Pacific had built

to attract the immigrants west
yet Mexicans who traveled north
& helped construct the lines
driving spikes in creosote-coated ties

had crossed against the law
unlike the Europeans entered through
New York & Galveston ports
mostly welcomed with open arms

if he not warmly received
found work at Sigal Hotel
washing dishes in its restaurant
in May would turn eighteen

described as quiet & pleasant
could communicate in basic English
but not enough to express
his passion for his waitress

A Rancher

his death didn't satisfy us
witnesses in front of him
standing on the platform planks
of the tall stockade-looking gallows
kept us from viewing him

Sheriff Irvin in a clear
solemn voice read the sentence
Judge Calhoun had pronounced before
when the jury found him
guilty in the first degree

at that time in November
a month after killing her
he had heard his punishment
& said it was right
that he wanted to die

on January 4th in handcuffs
he stepped forward to speak
his last words on earth
but waited until pressing forward
the crowd had quieted down

then unhesitating he calmly declared
he would unite with her
& after that it all
happened too fast as Sheriff
pulled tight on the rope

& the boy's body weight

when the trap door opened
dropped him down to where
few could see the deputies
by turns taking his pulse

on feeling none they informed
the Committee & sent word
to the Sheriff who took
a deep breath everyone heard
then let go the rope

but after the noose removed
not to leave a souvenir
he coiled & placed it
in the box with him
& hammered down its lid

the coffin on a wagon
the deputies seated on top
the Sheriff drove the horses
to Ross Cemetery's unmarked grave
as the crowd drifted away

we ranchers were all disgusted
for instead of being able
to string him up ourselves
the Sheriff had learned beforehand
we were riding into town

coming in from Eagle Cove
where the girl's parents lived
but before we could arrive
Sheriff took him to Abilene
& after returning to Baird

without his batting an eye
he said Vargas would receive
a fair & impartial trial
then headed home to sleep
while we ranted & raved

A Citizen

with the Clyde telephone wires
buzzing the news
a few of us commandeered
a T&P freight

took it east to the county seat
but in the night
a posse & buggy
bypassed us going back to the west

only at the station did we find
Sheriff Irvin & his men
had whisked away that spic
for safekeeping in Abilene

how could those lawmen
protect such scum
we should close the border
keep them from coming in

they only rape steal & murder
while we pay taxes
so their kids can attend
our expensive schools for free

they reproduce like rabbits
& speak no English
sure they work the fields
for very little pay

but they take jobs away
from those are legally here
I say ship them back
& put up a fence

Sheriff Al Irvin

Doc Grizzard feared
with his wounds
Alberto wouldn't survive
the 25 miles
from Baird to
Abilene's county jail

but I knew
if the mob
ever got aholt
of him he'd
surely swing from
the nearest tree

if he lived
to have his
day in court
it would do
right by him
& would protect

the town from
a reputation of
lawlessness by giving
proof that even
here in Baird
justice is served

besides the railroad
would have disapproved
would have shut
this junction down
as the company
threatened to do

when it sent
that Negro family
whose father operated

The Cowtown Circle

the coal chutes
& no one
ever bothered them

& they lived
here among us
without one incident
so I say
think first of
the community's good

The Jailor's Wife

once they brought him back to Baird
to await his trial
I chatted with him
on taking meals up to his cell

I saw a woman's presence comforted him
& began to feel
what a gentle spirit
resided there inside his skin & bones

couldn't conceive he did such a thing
it seemed he wouldn't
have harmed a fly
much less done it in cold blood

he never complained just spoke of her
& one time asked
for pencil & paper
& drew a beautiful picture of her

I let the custodian's children visit him
& he fashioned toys
from materials they brought
& he became a friend to them

their father told them when he died

& it saddened them
to lose their friend
who patiently listened to all their prattle

I told my husband of his sweetness
but he warned me
not to be naïve
to trust no man behind the bars

in his experience he had often seen
a woman would credit
anything a prisoner said
would even fall in love with him

one tried to help a prisoner escape
felt sorry for him
said don't be deceived
if he gets away he'll kill again

during his last hours his lawyer came
& with him too
was the Clyde priest
who spoke with & prayed with him

& then the Sheriff entered his cell
snapped around his wrists
two shiny new cuffs
below those of his jacket's faded sleeves

& wearing denim pants a blue shirt
& a dress tie
the priest beside him
he left to perform his final act

but just before he was taken away
he asked that I
for being so kind
be given his pencil drawing of her

Dallas Scarborough

since I had worked in Baird before
for my attorney-uncle B.L. Russell
just after being admitted to the bar
the Judge appointed me as counsel

of 200 murder cases the first I tried
I'd lose no other in my long career
at least by execution no client died
none sentenced more than 20 years

once I argued before the Appellate
& the Justices who heard that case
all favored moving the county seat
I lost the appeal & that courthouse

while I was studying law in Austin
I played baseball for the University
got a pro contract but turned it down
thought it beneath a lawyer's dignity

in football starred at defensive tackle
but 03-04 we won no championships
embarrassed by an all-Indian Haskell
but cannot compare to that case of his

as first coach at now Hardin-Simmons
I don't recall losing but a single game
that one a Big D parochial school won
but prefer that to such a grievous fame

from the first I knew we wouldn't win
for talking with him it was clear to me
I couldn't be successful defending him
not even on the grounds of his insanity

for he was thoughtful as a person can be
he told me he could not live without her
& on learning she was another's fiancée

had knifed her & himself to die together

if I had had even a little more experience
I was after all just six years older than he
I might have worked up a strong defense
but none would have convinced *that* jury

even though two men in Clyde had filed
for a change of venue based on prejudice
it was soon denied when the Sheriff held
there was not at all any evidence of such

but when I asked each prospective juror
whether he'd scruple in having to inflict
the death penalty each flint-eyed rancher
looked at him & replied "NOT A BIT!"

later it would become my firm convic-
tion that jurors can be depended upon
to deliver a fair just & honest verdict
& jury trial is democratic cornerstone

I would also conclude that every man
who's served on a jury the woman too
will thereon become a superior citizen
& even in his case it was probably true

but on that crisp morning 20 November
the courthouse halls & courtroom itself
overflowed with spectators all so eager
to watch in action law's avenging angel

after Judge Calhoun had called for order
& prosecution made its opening remarks
I pled his age even as I knew long before
it wouldn't change those minds or hearts

of 35 witnesses the State put on the stand
most swore they were in the dining room
& as she entered he had followed behind

pulled her about to stab her in the bosom

some recalled a terrified look on her face
when she saw him holding a paring knife
& all had heard a sudden frightened gasp
as she tried to break away & save her life

but just staggered & slumped to the floor
as each diner sat on entranced & hushed
while he jabbed at his chest over & over
until he fell on her when they all rushed

to her side but not feeling any heartbeat
a physician there gently closed her eyes
the bleeding boy then audibly breathed
& found alive was seized with outcries

dragged to the jail down Market Street
& as those witnesses had told & retold
their gruesome details no one believed
that jury to vote for life without parole

& so I'd decide not to have him testify
being certain then it would do no good
& in spite of the State's long testimony
by afternoon Judge Calhoun instructed

the jury to retire & consider the verdict
was never in doubt not for one moment
& in almost no time they returned with
guilty & their now-banned punishment

the Judge then called for Alberto to rise
& said if he wanted he now could speak
when all ears would listen with surprise
to his sincere voice though he still weak

from wounds by then had not yet healed
as he thanked the jury in broken English
for their decision was not to be appealed

since death not prison had been his wish

with the date set for execution it seemed
a load lifted from his shoulders as calm-
ly he stood up straight looking redeemed
& shook my hand but it wasn't any balm

for I have never lived down my only loss
since in all the cases I would later defend
a client served less time or had gotten off
& all the defendants I took were innocent

Zacatecas

for Baird had traded his birthplace
with its mines still active then
the Eden & Our Lady's Remedies
among richest in all New Spain
first worked when Chichimecans came
to dominate its hilly semi-desert terrain

its baroque cathedral of pink sandstone
built with gold & silver deposits
its Solomonic columns portals & naves
with sculpted Christ & Virgin Mary
& in flank niches Four Evangelists
cherubs caryatids vines & acanthus leaves

its plaza & winding cobbled streets
its alleyway called the Sad Indian
after its 1548 tale of Xolótl
who loved the last Chichimecan princess
while Xúchitl rejected him & wed
Gonzalo de Tolosa a Spanish captain

in the temple ruins of Tlacuitlapán
the desperate Xolótl watched from above
their procession to the Chapel Mexicapán

his faith lost in the gods
dying emaciated still holding a flower
the meaning of her Nahuatl name

starting place for missionaries' northern crusades
home to monasteries & a seminary
markets with leather crafts & silverworks
guavas grapes & the maguey's *aguamiel*
theatre opera house & teachers' college
at the cafes trumpeting mariachi bands

all exchanged for this little-known spot
passed through by cattle & rail
mostly just ranchers & antiquers stop
unlike his city where tourists arrive
to view the tribes & architecture
survive in its now UNESCO site

why then had he ever left
not from Revolution would only come
when Villa took its fortified hills
El Grillo & then La Bufa
Pancho's greatest victory over Federal troops
seven years after Vargas had hung

his complexion once noted as dark
though probably he wasn't an aborigine
not then ethnic nor drug-war refugee
it's said he'd received an education
his written Spanish correct & expressive
evident from letters addressed to her

not described as handsome or unattractive
no photo either confirms or denies
any comely girl of Hispanic blood
Zacatecan or a mixture of two
would have turned from his embrace
or did he seek another race

of the blonde & blue-eyed type

of lighter skins & thinner limbs
or instead of leaving for them
was it just for another place
or a job with decent pay
one with a future more secure

did he even intend to stay
or was he waiting to save
enough to continue north or east
to Fort Worth or further on
in search of his American dream
or was it just from wanderlust

& then while soaping the plates
he saw her with her tray
serving the customers food & drink
& after that no other plan
nothing else would count for him
but having her for his own

Emma Blakely

since she herself would never reveal
her feelings on her being attacked
her thoughts had she somehow known
of the reasons he would give
for his assault & attempted suicide
must rely on empathy to improvise:

in news of my sensational death
nearly nothing was written of me
besides my being active in church
attending Sunday school & Sunday service
& waiting on tables at Sigal's
nothing of my family or fiancé

to have them left in peace
& me buried in Eagle Cove
is all I would have wished

but in his pocket they found
letters he never passed to me
in a language I couldn't read

those have kept my memory alive
yet how could I ever accept
for having taken my life away
to live by his amorous words
tell of my figure attracted him
how I wounded his unworthy soul

gossip hinted the attention he paid
must have been amusing to me
but meeting him in the kitchen
I only smiled to be polite
too busy keeping up with orders
to take any notice of him

& besides I was happily engaged
to my Texas & Pacific brakeman
& we would soon be married
till suddenly he whirled me around
to face that blade he held
& plunged repeatedly into my breast

each time I shouted within myself
why do you hate me so
how ever imagine he worshipped me
& would try to slay himself
to be interred along with me
his cruel way of revering me

how believe in such a thing
no text I had ever read
no sermon I had ever heard
blessed a union based in sin
it would only belong in hell
never on earth or heaven above

how had I ever wronged him

never once did I encourage him
nor was ever unkind to him
how did I deserve to die
at the hands of a madman
I barely knew before that day

oh Scriptures teach us to forgive
those who have trespassed against us
how hard to learn that lesson
to put in practice His command
for each to love one another
as he did in murdering me

The Letters

my dearest love before your innocence
I'm a mean & rotten thing
I'm even worse than a dog
if you only knew the wounds
you open in my lonely soul
when you smile on another man

I am unworthy even to kiss
the earth your feet have touched
I'm beneath your blood & class
oh those are life's great differences
& rarely can we ever see
why our feelings come to us

what pain it gives to me
to tell you the horrible thought
has entered my head this night
the shock that it will cause
to your family & boarders here
oh such an awful bloody thought

I can already see your face
& can hardly bear its terror
it hurts & yet it fascinates

I know in this terrible affair
you will not believe my love
can mix good fortune with misery

you will think such a deed
can only have come from bitterness
not from the greatness of love
& yet the latter is true
for I have felt my dear
only the deepest devotion to you

oh my darling oh Emma mine
you are & will forever be
the dearest love life's given me
I wish you would understand me
& I could show to you
how little it means to me

to leave this always unfair world
since I'll die within your arms
your lips up close to mine
remembering how you smiled at me
how slender your arms & legs
yet unluckily not knowing the pain

your being would bring to me
though bitterness I have never felt
nor ever saw it in you
oh do know my virgin angel
for only a moment in life
I loved & adored you so

but finding you would marry another
jealousy would have reduced me to
a homeless bum on the street
oh who's to blame for this
my having to take your life
oh destiny it is destiny's fault

whenever you would glance at others

    I knew you would never return
    the looks I gave to you
    who knows what will happen now
    may our bodies remain as one
    hearts & souls in warming sun

       * * *

Baird October 19 1906

Mrs. Praxedïs Saldivar
Zacatecas

    dearest mother receive this final letter
    & grant your son your blessing
    you will never imagine my sorrow
    in having to tell you now
    by the time these words arrive
    I may lie under the earth

    do commend my soul to God
    & impart to the family members
    this news I send from Baird
    & with nothing further to say
    I here sign myself as ever
    your beloved loving son A Vargas

Epilogue

    once born in
    or moved to
    this Texas town

    one may choose
    to remain or
    leave as did

    Grandma when she
    took the kids

to Cowtown for

that city's benefits
Grandad staying for
his railway job

living it's said
here in a
shack until he

died while others
have stayed for
the place itself

its easy routine
its familiar scene
its bluebonnet springs

had Alberto left
once he learned
Emma loved another

& returned to
Zacatecas to waste
away holding in

his hand not
a knife but
as had Xolótl

a harmless flower
& let her
live her life

together with her
fiancé would his
future have held

any as precious
as she or

rather might he

in writing of
her & all
her charms have

come to discover
those of the
story or poem

had Daddy not
gone with Grandma
& married someone

other than Mom
would I then
not have been

not have seen
Chrisman & clippings
would lead to

the indebted lines
have tried reviving
their shortened lives

such questions come
without their answers
as surely Alberto

must have known
who wrote "anyone
is liable to

do it at
any time and
any moment—that

is if they
get into the

same fix that

I was in"
for even having
an answer right

one may fail
to follow through
& if not

to commit a
crime of passion
to sacrifice loved

instead of love

Acknowledgments

The Austin Chronicle: "After a Brief Illness"

The Dirty Goat: "After Álvaro Oyarzún's *El autodidacta,*" "Driving Across the Llano Estacado," "On Visiting NYC," and "Rondo for Mahler"

di-vêrsé-city: "María's Treatments"

Illya's Honey: "María's Smile"

Langdon Review of the Arts in Texas: "Annabella's Art," "Bees & Blue Salvia," "The Fastest Barber in the West," "A Grackle's-Eye View of Lakeline Mall," "María's Complaint," and "María's Hem"

Lightning Key Review: "Cedar vs. Live Oak"

Red River Review: "Jazz by the Boulevard," "María's Alstroemeria," "Ode to a '68 VW Bus," and "Out on a Limb,"

Sandhill Review: "March of the Penguins," "María's Heart," and "Of Burgers & Serpents"

The Southern Poetry Anthology, Vol. VIII: *Texas* (Texas Review Press, 2016): "Amaya's 'Dixie'"

The twenty concluding lines of "Jazz by the Boulevard" first appeared in Juliet George's *Camp Bowie Boulevard*, a volume in the Images of America series (Arcadia Publishing, 2013).

About Dave Oliphant

Born in 1939 in Fort Worth, Texas (known locally as Cowtown from its cattle auctions, abattoir, and packing plant), **Dave Oliphant** taught and/or edited a scholarly journal at the University of Texas at Austin from 1976 to 2006. A member of the Texas Institute of Letters, he won the TIL's 2011 Soeurette Diehl Fraser book translation award for his version of Chilean poet Nicanor Parra's *Discursos de sobremesa* (as *After-Dinner Declarations*). His series of poems entitled *Memories of Texas Towns & Cities* (begun in 1975 and completed in 2000) includes a 140-page poem on Austin that Michael King reported in *The Texas Observer* "takes its place . . . as a long poem in a modernist mode which makes an enduring contribution to the literature of its place, time, and country. And that's a great deal for any city to be proud of." Oliphant's most recent work is *Generations of Texas Poets* (Wings Press, 2015), a collection of his essays and reviews on Texas poetry, published over a 40-year period from 1973 to 2013.

www.ingramcontent.com/pod-product-compliance
Lightning Source LLC
Chambersburg PA
CBHW032034290426
44110CB00012B/795